T0383847

The
Monetary
Value
of **Time**

**Why Traditional
Accounting
Systems Make
Customers Wait**

The
Monetary
Value
of Time

Why Traditional Accounting Systems Make Customers Wait

Joyce I. Warnacut

CRC Press
Taylor & Francis Group
Boca Raton London New York

CRC Press is an imprint of the
Taylor & Francis Group, an **informa** business

A PRODUCTIVITY PRESS BOOK

CRC Press
Taylor & Francis Group
6000 Broken Sound Parkway NW, Suite 300
Boca Raton, FL 33487-2742

First issued in hardback 2019

© 2016 by Taylor & Francis Group, LLC
CRC Press is an imprint of Taylor & Francis Group, an Informa business

No claim to original U.S. Government works

ISBN-13: 978-1-4987-3713-5 (hbk)

Visit the Taylor & Francis Web site at
http://www.taylorandfrancis.com

and the CRC Press Web site at
http://www.crcpress.com

Contents

Author

Joyce I. Warnacut has over 30 years of experience in manufacturing firms serving as controller, CFO, and vice president. Warnacut is a graduate of Indiana University with a degree in accounting. She completed the requirements for her license as a certified public accountant in Wisconsin in 1983. Additionally, Warnacut completed the requirements for the APICS (The Association for Operations Management) certificate in production and inventory management in 1990. More recently, Warnacut attained the leadership level of certification in QRM (Quick Response Manufacturing) as awarded by Tempus Institute.

Warnacut currently serves as director of finance for Germanna Community College in Locust Grove, Virginia. In her previous recent tenure as CFO at Nicolet Plastics, Warnacut served as the chief architect for their QRM initiative, which culminated in Nicolet being awarded the Manufacturing Leader of 2013 for Operational Excellence by the Manufacturing Leadership Council (ML-100). By applying lead time reduction strategies, combined with transitioning from traditional efficiency and utilization metrics to time-based metrics, Nicolet was able to cut lead times by 66%, reduce finished goods inventory with improved turns (from 11 to 25 times per year), increase velocity three-fold, and grow both sales and bottom-line profits.

As CFO, Warnacut has championed Lean accounting concepts that include the elimination of standard costing, the development of a new model for product pricing and profitability, and has transformed the traditional standard cost-based financial statements to a simplified value-added format. A color-coded scorecard keeps the focus on time and aligns metrics with the organization's goals.

Warnacut has presented these concepts at national and international conferences, including Leadership Unleashed: Benchmarking Best Practices in Indianapolis, Indiana and the Annual Conference on Quick Response Manufacturing in Madison, Wisconsin. She is an advocate for a new way of thinking about accounting that challenges traditional cost accounting concepts.

Introduction

Every day we wait for something or someone. We wait in the doctor's office. We wait in traffic. We wait in the line at the check-out counter. In some cases, we wait *in a state in which we expect or hope something will happen soon*. In other cases, waiting makes us feel *temporarily neglected or unrealized*.

In today's world of instant gratification—instant news and instant food—we are not very good at waiting. A generation ago, it was accepted to wait days (or even weeks) for letters to arrive in the mail or for results to come back from a test or an election. Today, this is unnecessary and unacceptable. In these cases, waiting makes us feel *temporarily neglected or unrealized*.

We do not like to wait, and neither do our customers. We do not want our customers to feel neglected. But how do we eliminate the waiting? Can we afford to eliminate waiting? Won't it cost too much? Won't we have to hire too many people? Won't we have to buy too much equipment?

One place to start is by calculating wait time. If we work harder and do things faster, can we assume we will reduce wait time? If we keep our people and machines busy all the time, can we assume we will reduce wait time? What if we are looking in the wrong places?

Walk around your facility. Waiting happens in a lot of places. Do you see inventory of raw materials waiting to be processed into finished goods? Do you see inventory of work-in-process waiting for the next operation? Do you see finished goods inventory waiting to ship? Do you see piles of orders waiting for data entry? Do you see queues of quotes waiting for processing in the engineering department? Do you see customer orders waiting to be manufactured behind production of things that will go on the shelf? These are all examples of waiting that carry a cost and cause our customer to wait.

Unfortunately, our accounting systems and metrics often increase customers wait time rather than reduce it. Why is this? What can we do about it? Will we violate generally accepted accounting principles?

This book deals specifically with the pitfalls of traditional accounting systems and practices in a high-mix, low-volume manufacturing environment. The term *high-mix, low-volume* refers to many end products (specifications) produced in small batches. These are often custom products, meaning they are produced to the customer's specifications and may even be one-off, one-of-a-kind. The ability to deliver a product that is made to customer specifications, at a competitive price, in the quantity needed (rather than in large lots that have to be stocked), and at the same time quicker than the competitors is a distinct strategic advantage in many markets. However, traditional cost accounting systems will tell you that the process of creating strategic advantage in this fashion is not cost-effective.

The general practices today were developed in the era of assembly line production and economies of scale. In today's fast-paced world, with increasing demand for custom options and configure to order, traditional accounting methods can produce distorted information.

There are publications that discuss pitfalls of traditional accounting in a Lean manufacturing environment, proposing alternative *Lean accounting* treatments. The intent of this book is to expand the discussion beyond the world of Lean, which focuses on flow and level manufacturing load. A manufacturing environment with custom products in a high-mix, low-volume environment further compounds the issues raised by Lean accounting advocates. If overhead allocation skews results in a Lean environment, it is almost certain to misstate results in a high-mix, low-volume environment with varying flow rates and lot sizes.

How much would it be worth to your customer—and your business— if you could eliminate the waiting and get the product in the customers' hands quicker? Is your accounting system telling you what you need to know to drive both bottom-line results and customer responsiveness? How do you put a value on waiting? How do you justify the addition of people and equipment to eliminate waiting? How do you measure progress? What metrics measure the value of time?

These are the questions to be explored in this book.

Portugese proverb

Money is not gained by losing time.

1

Net Present Value: Just the Tip of the Iceberg

 Definition of the *Time Value of Money*

The idea that money available at the present time is worth more than the same amount in the future due to its potential earning capacity. This core principle of finance holds that, provided money can earn interest, any amount of money is worth more the sooner it is received. The value today, of cash or cash flows to be received in the future, is called *net present value*, abbreviated as NPV.

$$\text{NPV}(i, N) = \sum_{t=0}^{N} \frac{R_t}{(1+i)^t}$$

where
  t is the time of the cash flow
  i is the rate of return that could be earned on an investment in the financial markets with similar risk; the opportunity cost of capital
  N is the total number of periods
  R_t is the net cash flow, that is, cash inflow minus cash outflow, at time t

One finance formula that does acknowledge the value of time is NPV. Present value is simply the sum of a series of cash flows over time in terms of present dollars. It factors in inflation and what you could make investing your money elsewhere. This formula applies an interest rate based on the assumption that money today is worth more than money tomorrow. This is the accounting version of "a bird in the hand is worth two in the bush."

The formula is regularly applied to evaluate a series of returns on an investment—typically equipment—to incorporate a time value associated with the immediate outflow of funds and the periodic inflow of savings generated by the investment. What if we applied this same concept to shortening the time our customers have to wait for their product?

Assume that we have a customer who buys $1,000,000 worth of product each year. Our cost is $900,000, which generates $100,000 profit per year. The manufacturing process is intensive, and we spend the whole year producing the product that is delivered in one annual shipment. What if we were able to improve our processes and deliver quarterly shipments of $250,000? How about monthly shipments of $100,000?

Using an interest rate of 5%, the analysis is shown in Figures 1.1 through 1.3.

If we buy our raw materials of $900,000 up front and make one sale per year of $1,000,000, the net present value of our investment at a rate of 5% is $52,381 (Figure 1.1). If we buy 1/4 of our materials at the start of each quarter and ship every 90 days, we will yield $25,000 per quarter based on $250,000 of sales less $225,000 of materials. The present value of our investment at a rate of 5% is $86,303 (Figure 1.2). If we buy our materials at the start of each month, and ship every 30 days, we yield $8,333 per month based on $83,333 of sales less $75,000 of materials. The present value of our investment at a rate of 5% is $97,809 (Figure 1.3). Simply by shortening the cycle between buying materials and shipping product, we have generated an additional value of $45,428 ($97,809 − $52,381).

Discount rate	5%
Days in year	365
NPV	52,380.95
Date	**Value**
1/1/14—buy materials for annual supply	(900,000.00)
12/31/14—sell product	1,000,000.00

FIGURE 1.1
The net present value of annual shipments.

Discount rate	5%
Days in year	365
NPV	86,302.81
Date	**Value**
1/1/14—buy materials for 90 day supply	(225,000.00)
4/1/14—sell product and buy more material for net $25,000 inflow	25,000.00
7/1/14—sell product and buy more material for net $25,000 inflow	25,000.00
10/1/14—sell product and buy more material for net $25,000 inflow	25,000.00
12/31/14—sell product	250,000.00

FIGURE 1.2
The net present value of quarterly shipments.

Discount rate	5%
Days in year	365
NPV	97,808.55
Date	**Value**
1/1/14—buy materials for 30 day supply	(75,000.00)
2/1/14—sell product and buy more material for net $8,333 inflow	8,333.33
3/1/14—sell product and buy more material for net $8,333 inflow	8,333.33
4/1/14—sell product and buy more material for net $8,333 inflow	8,333.33
5/1/14—sell product and buy more material for net $8,333 inflow	8,333.33
6/1/14—sell product and buy more material for net $8,333 inflow	8,333.33
7/1/14—sell product and buy more material for net $8,333 inflow	8,333.33
8/1/14—sell product and buy more material for net $8,333 inflow	8,333.33
9/1/14—sell product and buy more material for net $8,333 inflow	8,333.33
10/1/14—sell product and buy more material for net $8,333 inflow	8,333.33
11/1/14—sell product and buy more material for net $8,333 inflow	8,333.33
12/1/14—sell product and buy more material for net $8,333 inflow	8,333.33
12/31/14—sell product	83,333.33

FIGURE 1.3
The net present value of monthly shipments.

The important concept is to look closely at the time line, from the point the order is received to the point where the cash is collected. Any reduction in this time line will improve customer responsiveness *and* cash flow at the same time.

Therefore, not only does the customer get accelerated delivery, we also add value by using our money more efficiently and turning it faster. This is the money value of time, and the foundation of velocity.

In the chapters to come, you will discover that the one time-based cost that accountants recognize, the time value of money, is only the tip of the iceberg. Time is a *lot* more money than just the cost of capital. Accounting does not put a value on the cost of waiting and queues. Nor does it value the cost of consuming resources to produce things that cannot be quickly converted to cash. In each of the examples above, the product cost is reported as 90% with a 10% profit margin, even though there is a vast difference in cash velocity and customer responsiveness between the options.

2

Velocity Improves Productivity and Working Capital

 Velocity

Velocity is a measurement of the rate and direction of motion. It measures both speed and direction. In business terms, this means not only shortening response times, but also doing so by making the correct directional decisions.

Velocity may be the most neglected, and at the same time, the most important financial metric of our time. In *Execution: The Discipline of Getting Things Done* by Larry Bossidy and Ram Charan (2002), the impact of velocity is discussed as follows:

> Building to order means producing a unit after the customer's order is transmitted to the factory. The system squeezes time out of the entire cycle from order to delivery. This system minimizes inventory at both ends of the pipeline, incoming and outgoing. Building-to-order improves inventory turnover, which increases asset velocity, one of the most underappreciated components of making money. Velocity is the ratio of sales dollars to net assets deployed in the business (plant and equipment, inventories, and AR minus AP). Higher velocity improves productivity and reduces working capital. It also improves cash flow, the life blood of any business, and can help improve margins as well as revenue and market share.

The more time we squeeze out of the process, the more attractive make to order becomes. Just think about the financial impact of eliminating forecast errors, obsolete inventory, and reducing warehouse space requirements! Lower inventories also improve the accuracy of financial reporting, because as you eliminate inventory, you also eliminate the magnitude of valuation errors caused by poor cutoffs, incorrect cost data, and incorrect perpetual inventory levels. We need to break through the thinking that *small runs are bad* and move to matching production to demand. Dell revolutionized the computer industry with their assemble-to-order business model and 80 inventory turns per year. As our response time decreases, the need to make ahead also diminishes. Manufacturers that consider inventory to be business as usual need to ask, "What would it take to eliminate inventory? What changes in my process, my perceptions, and my systems would be required to make all of my products to order?"

Business velocity refers to a company's ability to generate operational speed while heading in the right direction. Operational speed does not necessarily mean working faster; it means that all waste, waiting, and unnecessary activities are eliminated from the process. The right direction means that the activities to save time and eliminate waiting must be focused on the activities that will make the greatest impact on overall customer response time. This requires that focus is put on processes or operations that are on the critical path. In other words, does the compression of time in the process reduce overall lead time? In order to determine this, the business process must be mapped to determine where the greatest opportunities lie. While many mapping tools exist, one tool that clearly incorporates time is the concept of MCT (manufacturing critical Path time) as presented by Rajan Suri (2010). MCT is a time-based metric that defines lead time in a precise way so that it properly quantifies an organization's total system-wide waste.

2.1 MEASURING LEAD TIME

An MCT map is a graphic representation of the flow of an order through the specified subset of an organization. The flow is from left to right, and the representation is intuitive, as seen in this example.

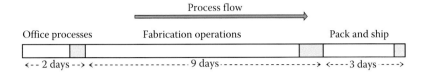

FIGURE 2.1
Example of an MCT map.

Figure 2.1 shows an MCT map for an order from receipt at a company until the order is loaded onto a truck for shipping. In this example, sales activities and processes prior to the receipt of an order are not shown; also not shown are any processes used in the shipping and logistics after the order leaves the company. This illustrates that the scope of an MCT map is typically limited to a subset of an enterprise, as required for the goals of a specific project. In Figure 2.1, the MCT for this subset is 14 days (= 2 + 9 + 3).

Gray space illustrates the total time when *someone is actually working on the order*, as shown by the rectangles with the shaded gray. These are customarily placed at the *end* of the operations for which this time occurs. For instance, the order spends 9 days in Fabrication Operations, and the Gray Space can be seen at the end of this 9-day segment. Experience with hundreds of projects in manufacturing companies has shown that Gray Space is typically less than 5% of MCT.

White space illustrates the remaining time spent by the order in a particular area; this is the time when *nothing is happening to the order*! This is customarily placed before the Gray Space for the same area. Looking at the Fabrication Operations again, you can see the White Space preceding the Gray Space. Although White Space is typically 95% or more of the total lead time, traditional cost-reduction or efficiency-improvement approaches focus on reducing the working time for processing jobs. Since the Gray Space is a tiny fraction of the MCT, such approaches typically have limited impact on overall lead time (Suri, 2014).

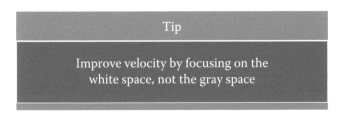

Tip

Improve velocity by focusing on the
white space, not the gray space

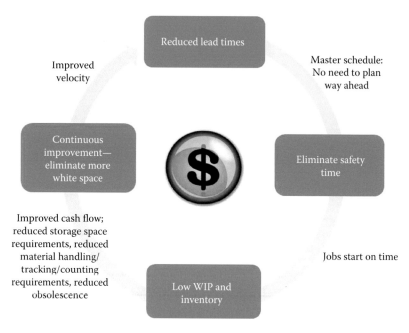

Improved velocity

Reduced lead times

Master schedule: No need to plan way ahead

Continuous improvement—eliminate more white space

Eliminate safety time

Improved cash flow; reduced storage space requirements, reduced material handling/ tracking/counting requirements, reduced obsolescence

Jobs start on time

Low WIP and inventory

FIGURE 2.2
Response time accelerator.

The good news is that since white space is commonly 95% or more of total lead time, there is a tremendous opportunity for a targeted continuous improvement program. If you target the largest areas of white space, incredible results are possible. This creates what might be called the *Response Time Accelerator,* which is the inverse of the *Response Time Spiral* described in *It's About Time* (Figure 2.2).

2.2 MEASURING VELOCITY

MCT, as described in detail in the books by Suri, is an excellent measure of customer responsiveness, that is, the ability to respond quickly to a customer with made-to-order products. Time is money, yet MCT alone does not measure the contribution—or the value added—of products. The combination of speed and contribution is extremely powerful in terms of bottom-line results. So how do we measure velocity in terms of dollars?

Most companies spend inordinate amounts of time looking at gross margins. This includes enormous effort on the part of management and cost accounting to determine the margin generated by unit, which requires calculating the full product cost (materials, labor, and overhead) of each product compared to the selling price. However, margins alone ignore the impact of speed. A product that generates half the margin may be just as profitable if it moves through the production process twice as fast. Conversely, high-margin products will not deliver a superior return if they are offset by slow production throughput (Rothschild, 2006).

By combining margin formulas and throughput formulas, a more meaningful measure of how products generate returns can be developed:

- Contribution Margin = Profit/Unit (Contribution Margin = Revenue – Variable Cost)
- Production Throughput = Units/Hour (Hours = Production Hours including Set Up Time)
- Return per Hour of Production = Contribution Margin per Hour of Production

If you combine these formulas, algebraically the units cancel and the combined measure of both margin *and* throughput is Profit per Production Time (hour, minute, week, or month) (Figure 2.3).

This definition of throughput per time, or contribution over a unit of time, is not new. It is covered extensively in the book *Throughput Accounting* by Thomas Corbett (1998). The definition has value, because it puts into perspective the fact that profit margins alone do

FIGURE 2.3
Measure of contribution and throughput.

FIGURE 2.4
Measure of contribution and lead time.

not tell the whole story. When time is incorporated into the formula, product profitability can change dramatically.

In addition to production throughput, there is another dimension to time in a manufacturing concern. What if it takes weeks, or months, for an order to go through the factory? Or worse yet, what if the plant, or cell, achieves maximum throughput only to put product on the shelf? In both these situations, resources in the form of material and labor have been consumed. However, they have been consumed making things that cannot be immediately converted to cash. Did this consumption of resources delay the production of other products, or purchase of other materials, that could have been converted to cash more rapidly?

The real measure of velocity is how quickly an order is converted to cash. Using the definition of MCT, an even better measure of how products generate cash *and* return can be developed (Figure 2.4):

- Contribution Margin = Profit/Unit (Contribution Margin = Revenue – Variable Cost)
- MCT = Units/Day (Days = Days from Receipt of Order to Shipment)
- Return per Day of Lead Time = Contribution Margin per Day of Lead Time

If you combine these formulas, algebraically the units cancel and the combined measure of both margin *and* lead time is Profit per Lead Time (hour, minute, week, or month).

Higher velocity coupled with profit margin equals the true return on sales. So a company's success is dependent upon *the combination of*

Should we sell more of "A" at a 20% margin, or "B" at a 10%t margin?

	Product A	Product B
Revenue	$1,000	$1,000
Material	$800	$900
Contribution	$200	$100
Margin %	20%	10%
Production hours	4	1
Contribution per production hours	$50	$100
MCT days	20	5
Contribution per day of MCT	$10.00	$20.00

FIGURE 2.5
Margin ignores time.

operational speed *and* profit margin on the products sold. The higher the velocity, the greater the total profit or return on sales.

Velocity, and the associated increase in throughput, increases volume with the same fixed costs. Throughput focuses on process time through the entire system, not one particular machine, department, or operation.

Consider the following example shown in Figure 2.5. Product A and Product B both sell for $1,000. Product A has a $200 margin, or 20%. Product B has a $100 margin, or 10%. Traditional thinking says we should sell more of Product A. However, is this true if Product A takes twice as long to make as Product B? Is this true if Product A takes four times as long to convert to cash?

When you consider the impact on return on sales *plus* the impact on cash flow (refer to Chapter 1), organizations cannot afford to ignore the potential bottom-line impact of saving time and generating operational speed (Figure 2.5 and Box 2.1).

BOX 2.1   VELOCITY IN ACTION

One business I worked for was generating 40% bottom-line pre-tax income on every dollar of revenue in an industry that was considered commodity, and competitors were having trouble turning a profit at all. The secret? Velocity. While others were building to forecast, quoting long lead times, and attempting to schedule all of this in their ERP systems, this company did the following:

- Suppliers delivered raw materials daily.
- Any order could go to production in 24 h or less after receipt.
- Scheduling was done one shift at a time rather than scheduling (and rescheduling) orders weeks out.
- All production was to order; the orders were packed and ready for shipment at the end of the production line.
- Much of the time, the order went straight to the shipping dock rather than into storage.
- Total MCT (lead time) of 36 h.

The result?

- Minimal raw material and finished goods inventory. (A complete physical count took one person about 2 h.)
- Over 50 inventory turns per year for both raw materials and finished goods.
- Minimal requirements for inventory personnel, material handlers, cycle counters, and so on.
- Minimal warehouse storage space requirements.
- No inventory picking errors.
- 99.9% on time delivery rates.
- No inventory obsolescence.
- No forecast errors.
- No rescheduling for order changes, schedule changes, and equipment downtime.
- Positive cash flow.
- Profits far in excess of the industry norm.

The business model made all the difference. The more streamlined the process, the less time required for upfront planning (and replanning) before production begins. Voila! Velocity!

3

Case Study:
Velocity Impact on Results

> *Throughput* is the amount of work that can be performed or the amount of output that can be produced by a system in a given period of time.

For an 8-year period, I served as a CFO of a manufacturer of custom injection-molded plastic parts. Injection molders have historically favored long runs to minimize mold changes. Parts that have wide tolerances and low-quality thresholds are also favored, as they require less labor. These biases were created by utilization and efficiency mindsets. In other words, the more machines you have running, the better—because your utilization numbers will improve. More setups are bad because setup time cuts into run time and will lower your utilization. Lower labor requirements will lower your cost. There are some fundamental problems with these assumptions:

- These numbers do not measure bottom-line results. Running more does not guarantee more profit. Using less labor on a particular item does not guarantee that the item contributes more to the bottom line than another product that uses more labor. The materials and labor required *relative to price and run time* determine the impact on the bottom line.
- These numbers do not measure contribution over time. Is a 40 h run that generates a contribution of $400 ($10 per hour) to be valued over a 10 h run that generates the same $400 ($40 per hour)?

- The numbers ignore interrelationships and systems dynamics. What is the impact on other jobs in queue behind the 40 h job that are waiting for the same piece of equipment?

To illustrate these concepts, employees were presented with two different 8 h schedules. Each schedule was composed of parts that had actually run over the previous 2 weeks. On one schedule were the *favored* jobs, consuming 90 h of machine time and requiring five setups. This schedule was the *S&S Team* (Shoot and Ship). On another schedule were the *bad* jobs, consuming 83 h of machine time and requiring 12 setups. This schedule was the *R&R Team* (Rapid & Responsive). When employees were asked which team they wanted to be on, the majority preferred the S&S Team.

Employees were then presented with actual data that showed the results in terms of sales and profit sharing (based on bottom line contribution) if each shift ran that mix of products for an entire year. The results, based on real items, prices, and cost data, are shown in Figure 3.1.

What was the reason for the difference in results? The R&R team capitalized on strategic variability. The products in the mix for the S&S team were commodities. They involved standard materials, simple processes that are easily duplicated, had high volumes, and as a result were easily quoted by any and all injection molders. Consequently, pricing was very competitive and margins were low. However, the products in the R&R team involved a complex mix of engineered materials, complex processes, and low volumes. These products command a higher price, and the field of competitors is limited. The ability to take on and manage the complexity commands a premium.

Many companies focus on eliminating the complexity created by many materials, complicated processes, and varying run sizes because of the systems and controls required to manage the diversity. However, when a

S&S team	R&R team
• Sales/shift = $6,000	• Sales/shift = $20,000
• Annual sales = $4.5 million	• Annual sales = $15 million
• Profit sharing/shift = $50	• Profit sharing/shift = $1,000
• Annual profit sharing = $37,500	• Annual profit sharing = $750,000

FIGURE 3.1
Results for the *S&S* vs. *R&R* teams.

conscious decision is made to capitalize on the diversity of high-mix and low-volume products as a business strategy, the perspective changes.

The teams were aware that the products on the R&R team were more complex, requiring significantly more time and effort in set up, processing, and quality control. However, they were not aware of how well the company was compensated for providing that expertise.

When asked a second time which team they wanted to be on, the vote changed quite a bit. Of course, manufacturers are not always at liberty to pick and choose product mix; however, the message that utilization and efficiency do not necessarily translate to bottom-line results is clear. The final questions for the group:

- Which team is the most flexible?
- Which approach results in the lower inventory?
- Which team will have the quicker response time?
- Which team would our customers want serving them?

Unanimously, the answer was the Rapid & Responsive (R&R) Team.

4

Product Cost

4.1 THE END AND THE MEANS: WHY DO WE COST PRODUCTS?

At first blush, this seems like a simple question with a simple answer. We need to know what it costs us to make a product for a lot of reasons. We need to know if we are making money. We need to know how to price it. We need to value inventory. We need to decide if we can out-source it cheaper than we can make it. We need to know if we are making it efficiently.

The fact that there are so many answers to this question is precisely the problem. The cost to value inventory may not be the same cost needed for other purposes, such as that needed to determine if we are making money on the product. The fact that generally accepted accounting principles (GAAP) require absorbed costs in order to *value inventory* has resulted in fully absorbed costs being used for many other purposes for which they are misleading.

What to do? Do we need to keep two cost systems? Some businesses do, but it is not necessary to do so. If cost data is more important for decision making and profitability analysis, then the focus should first and foremost be on the cost data that serves that purpose. There are numerous options, some of which are detailed later in this text, for valuing inventory that do not require fully absorbed costing at the item level. This requires a new way of thinking. How do I want to see my costs? What are my true variable costs? How can I get my cost system to give me this cost and still meet requirements of GAAP? Focus first on the ends, then the means.

> ### Tip
> Always keep in mind what you are going to use the cost for. The objective should determine the most effective product cost approach.

4.2 ABSORPTION VERSUS VARIABLE COSTING

Absorption Costing

Definition: The practice of unitizing manufacturing overhead as a product cost along with variable cost.

A quick overview of absorption product costing and variable product costing is necessary to begin to see the pitfalls in traditional product costing that might result in making customers wait. Absorption costing refers to the inclusion of all costs associated with manufacturing a particular product in the cost base, which includes both direct costs and overhead costs. Variable costing includes only costs that vary directly with production in product cost. Factory overhead is accounted for as an expense in the period in which it is incurred, rather than being charged to the product cost.

Absorption costing is the only method recognized by the Financial Accounting Standards Board as acceptable for externally published financial statements. Absorption costing is also required by the Internal Revenue Service in tax preparation. The requirement for fully absorbed costs applies specifically to inventory valuation and reporting. Accounting academics are quick to point out that fully absorbed product costs and GAAP apply to financial accounting and not necessarily managerial accounting. However, in practice, the difficulty of maintaining multiple cost systems results in one system being used for both purposes most of the time. Additionally, the wide availability of product cost data on Enterprise Resource Planning (ERP) systems (out to six decimal places) causes the assumption that it must be correct and can be used for any kind of analysis.

> ### Accuracy or Precision?
>
> Don't make the mistake of confusing precision with accuracy. Just because the cost system calculates product cost out to six decimal places doesn't mean the cost is accurate.

Under absorption costing, inventory values must include the related cost of materials, labor, and overhead used to produce the inventory. Those costs will go into inventory and will not hit the bottom line until the inventory is sold. This is an application of the matching principle, theoretically matching the cost of the sale with the revenue produced.

Under variable costing (also referred to as direct costing) only the costs that vary directly with production are capitalized or charged to inventory. Fixed manufacturing costs are expensed in the period incurred. Variable costing would typically define variable costs as material, direct labor, and possibly some manufacturing overhead expenses that fluctuate with volume. Fixed overhead expenses are charged in the period incurred, rather than being capitalized in the cost of inventory. This is why the use of variable costing is said to better approximate cash flow, since more costs are expensed in the period they are incurred, rather than recording the costs in inventory, which makes them an asset and eliminates the impact on the bottom line until such time as the product is sold. This creates a mismatch between the month the cash goes out and the month the expense is actually recorded.

Variable cost proponents point out the erroneous assumption that users of fully absorbed cost data often make, which is that if they stop making a product, the overhead cost will also stop. In other words, if my cost is $10 a unit, and I generally make 10 units a month for a cost of $100; if I stop making these units does my cost go down by $100? In fact, the answer is no. The fixed costs are still there! Cost behavior is better analyzed—and predicted—when using only those costs that can be proven to vary directly with production levels. Although an accountant may be well aware of the distinction between variable and fixed components in product cost, the other users of that data—operations, sales, and engineering, for example—may not be as well versed and often assume that the cost for any product is, in fact, the cost. In turn, product margin (sales price minus cost) is also widely used for pricing and profitability analysis without regard to fixed and variable components.

When comparing the two methods, it is often said that full absorption encourages inventory growth. This occurs because income can be increased by putting more products into inventory. At the time the inventory is made, the production costs do not hit the bottom line. Rather, they are *stashed* in inventory. The costs are recorded at the time the product is sold. However, there is no penalty from a product cost standpoint related to the time in inventory, and when it is sold the cost is unchanged. If the product ends up as unsaleable due to obsolescence or design revisions, the cost will then be recognized as a total loss—even though it boosted your income in the month it was put in inventory.

Related to this discussion is the concept of *sunk cost*. In economic and business decision making, sunk costs are retrospective (past) costs that have already been incurred and cannot be recovered. Sunk costs are sometimes contrasted with *prospective costs*, which are future costs that may be incurred or changed if an action is taken. Both retrospective and prospective costs may be either fixed (i.e., they are not dependent on volume) or variable (dependent on volume).

In traditional economic theory, only prospective (future) costs are relevant to an investment decision. Sunk costs should not influence a decision, because doing so does not rationally assess a decision on its own merits. Evidence suggests this theory fails to predict real-world behavior. Sunk costs do affect decisions, because humans are loss averse. For example, you may choose not to purchase a new machine, on its own merits and with a good payback, because you already have a machine that is not fully utilized. One example of sunk cost is equipment expenditures, as the equipment has already been purchased and the purchase price (and depreciation expense) cannot be altered. Another example would be rent under a lease agreement, which again, cannot be changed under the terms and duration of the lease. Both of these examples would be considered overhead. Both would factor into overhead rates and allocations in traditional accounting. Therefore, investment decisions and make or buy decisions using product cost data containing this data are erroneous (often referred to as the *sunk cost fallacy*).

The management accounting practices in use today, based on fully absorbed product costs, were developed by 1925 and have changed very little over the past 90 years. Take for example, the opening paragraph of *Relevance Lost: The Rise and Fall of Management Accounting*: "Today's management accounting information, driven by the procedures and cycle of the organization's financial reporting system, is too late, too aggregated, and too distorted to be relevant for managers' planning and control decisions" (Johnson and Kaplan, 1987). This book was published in 1987 by the Harvard Business School Press to critical acclaim and was the 1989 winner of the American Accounting Association's Notable Contribution to Management Accounting Literature Award. And yet, 27 years after the publication of *Relevance Lost*, cost accounting practices remain much the same as in 1925.

Why are 90-year-old practices so ingrained in modern manufacturing enterprises? It is due to a combination of factors that create a self-perpetuating cycle. Businesses have legacy systems, reports, and practices based on *we've always done it this way*. Automated accounting systems are designed to accommodate the business practices of its users, while at the same time meeting the requirements of GAAP. Universities and colleges teach good old-fashioned cost accounting because businesses still use it. Businesses have a difficult time changing the cost model when their systems do not support the new way of thinking, and when their accountants have no experience and minimal training in alternative cost approaches. And so it goes. The cycle will continue until business owners and stakeholders demand something different from their software developers, educators, and accountants.

Change should be motivated by the divergence of current manufacturing from the assembly line or repetitive manufacturing model; and the emergence of the customized, high-mix manufacturing model. As pointed out in *Relevance Lost*, historically academic researchers have concentrated on "elegant and sophisticated approaches to analyze costs for single-product, single-process firms" without considering implementation in today's organizations with "hundreds or thousands of products and with complex, multistage production processes." Indeed, an analysis of course descriptions for the required accounting curricula of five major universities in the Big 10 found limited mention of *Lean accounting* or similar alternative accounting treatments. Most offer traditional cost accounting courses, with some reference to Just-In-Time, Total Quality Management, and Activity-Based Costing (ABC) as subjects covered in the course.

If discussed at all, alternatives to traditional product costing are a very small portion of the required cost accounting course. One widely used textbook does mention *Lean accounting* and *simplified accounting,* but the actual text on these subjects consists of less than 30 pages of an 800 page textbook. If, in fact, management accounting has lost all relevance as a measure of an organization's operations, does not the study of alternative accounting methods and how they support current manufacturing strategies deserve an entire course, rather than just a chapter or two?

Another source of the difficulty of changing cost models can be found in ERP systems in wide use today. The cost modules of these systems are widely based on fully absorbed cost (often in the form of standard cost) and generally offer the user multiple options for how to allocate overhead, but none even consider the fact that allocating overhead to product cost—in any fashion—may not provide meaningful information and may even be counterproductive. The dashboards and standard reports that come with these systems also focus on utilization and efficiency, which are metrics built around traditional product cost theory. Enterprises use the cost methods and reporting options that are available within their accounting modules as *best practice* and the ERP accounting system dictates the method, rather than the method being selected based on the production environment, product characteristics, and business model.

The underlying theory of fully absorbed product cost is that the specific cost of any end item can be classified into one of three categories of cost, either material, labor, or overhead:

- Material costs can be determined by calculating the quantity and cost of the material used to manufacture any item, typically as specified in the bill of material (BOM).
- Direct labor costs can be calculated by timing operators at each process step. The assumption is that if you do not run production, you do not incur direct labor costs and that direct labor can be controlled; that is, turned off and on as production starts and stops.
- Overhead can be specified on a per unit basis by allocating the entire pool of cost to items.

There are many approaches to overhead allocation, including separating variable and fixed components, defining multiple allocation methods and denominators based on cost drivers, and developing separate cost pools.

By far the most common and widely used approach for allocations is volume based. Some surveys estimate that 40% or more of firms rely on traditional volume-based allocation systems (Balakrishnan et al., 2012a). Volume-based allocations allocate overhead expenses by dividing by an expected number of hours to be consumed. Hours are typically expressed in terms of machine hours or direct labor hours. Figure 4.1 is an example of volume-based allocations for $10,000,000 of overhead and three products (hours could be either labor or machine hours).

Now assume that through Process Improvement activities, the time to produce Product A is cut in half, from 10 to 5 h (Figure 4.2).

In other words, the cost of all *three* products just went up because of *improved* throughput on one part, because the overhead rate has increased from $50 to $67 per hour. In reality, both revenue and overhead are unchanged. Based on the $50 per hour rate, because we only used 150,000 h, the absorption of costs to products was $50 per hour × 150,000 h = $7,500,000. This means we are $2,500,000 short of absorbing our $10,000,000 of overhead across our parts. In accounting terms, we are "under-absorbed." In cost accounting terms, *under-absorption* is the cost of unused capacity. Therefore, the motivation is to increase the

$10,000,000 to be allocated	Product A	Product B	Product C	Total
(1) Number of parts	10,000	10,000	10,000	30,000
(2) Hours per part	10	6	4	
Total hours 1 × 2	100,000	60,000	40,000	200,000
Overhead rate per hour				$50.00

FIGURE 4.1
Volume-based overhead allocations.

$10,000,000 to be allocated	Product A	Product B	Product C	Total
(1) Number of parts	10,000	10,000	10,000	30,000
(2) Hours per part	5	6	4	
Total hours 1 × 2	50,000	60,000	40,000	150,000
Overhead rate per hour				$66.67

FIGURE 4.2
Volume-based overhead allocation after process improvement.

denominator (make more) which will lower cost and consume the total capacity.

As an answer to this issue, some cost accounting formulas use *practical capacity* as the denominator. Practical capacity is an output level (whether machine hours, labor hours, pounds, barrels, etc.) that is less than theoretical capacity. This allows for some flexibility in the processes, as well as allowing time for maintenance, downtime, setups, and so on. While this is certainly preferable to using an unrealistic target of 100%, it still can motivate counterproductive measures to consume under-absorbed capacity. Most of all, it still does not align production with orders. Rather, it motivates a fixed amount of production regardless of orders, while allowing some cushion.

In a make-to-order business, misalignment of production and orders is disastrous. The motivation should be to make exactly the number of units you have orders for. Making any more is consuming unnecessary resources—materials, labor, space, and cash. However, the cost world does not recognize the cost of resources that have been consumed for inventory that does not have an associated order any differently than those that have been consumed to produce parts that can be converted to cash immediately. In fact, by *absorbing* these costs into inventory, we avoid recording these expenses, thereby increasing income. Therefore, the practice of recording these costs on our balance sheet in inventory rather than expensing them as they are incurred actually incentivizes increasing inventory!

When the allocation basis is direct labor hours, the motivation is to keep everyone busy regardless of demand. If you do not convert the *standard* amount of resources into your product every month, you will be under-absorbed. When the allocation basis is machine hours, the motivation is to keep your machines running, regardless of demand. In either case, if you do not convert the *standard* amount of resources into your product every month, you will be under-absorbed. It appears as if your costs have gone up, since you need to increase your rates in order to fully absorb your overhead.

> **Common Cost Misconception**
>
> You can lower costs by producing more.

Most systems rely on budgeted volumes (typically on an annual basis) as the basis for overhead rates. To come up with the hours over which costs are to be spread, one needs estimates of demand, product mix, and capacity. Even with the use of sophisticated modeling techniques and mathematical analyses, it is very difficult to predict both volumes and mix in any certainty a year out. This is compounded even further when the mix involves many end items and also when the volumes are segregated into pools or work centers.

4.2.1 Applicability of Fully Absorbed Cost Models to High-Mix, Low-Volume Environments

Adding more complexity (and reality), let us consider the use of overhead rate calculations in a high mix, nonrepetitive environment. Since it is rarely as simple as one machine and one product, it is more likely that there are a pool of indirect costs that must be allocated over many products, machines, and work centers.

In order to properly allocate overhead, the manufacturer must determine a rate for each machine/work center/department. These rates are generally determined based on the relative investment of equipment in a particular work center and/or historical expenses that are specific to that work center. Assume that we have four functional work centers:

1. Machining
2. Welding
3. Heat treating
4. Assembly

The manufacturer has determined that machining should get 35% of the allocation, welding and heat treating 25% each, and assembly the remaining 15%. Using these numbers, the $10 million of overhead will be applied to products made in each work center as shown (Figure 4.3).

If we assume that the manufacturer saves the same 50% of hours required on Product A by eliminating the need to machine or weld the part by adding additional assembly time, then the cost structure has changed as follows (Figure 4.4).

Due to saving *time,* the cost of both machining and welding has gone up. Assembly rates have actually decreased by virtue of adding hours. In reality, have the fixed costs of any of the work centers actually

$10 million to be allocated	Machining	Weld	Heat treat	Assembly	Total
Product A hours	50,000	30,000		20,000	100,000
Product B hours	6,000		6,000	48,000	60,000
Product C hours	8,000	8,000	12,000	12,000	40,000
Total hours	64,000	38,000	18,000	80,000	200,000
% of total	35%	25%	25%	15%	100%
Overhead $	$3,500,000	$2,500,000	$2,500,000	$1,500,000	$10,000,000
Rate per hour	$54.69	$65.79	$138.89	$18.75	$50.00

FIGURE 4.3
Volume-based overhead allocations by work center.

$10 million to be allocated	Machining	Welding	Heat treat	Assembly	Total
Product A hours	0	0		50,000	50,000
Product B hours	6,000		6,000	48,000	60,000
Product C hours	8,000	8,000	12,000	12,000	40,000
Total hours	14,000	8,000	18,000	110,000	150,000
Overhead $	$3,500,000	$2,500,000	$2,500,000	$1,500,000	$10,000,000
Rate per hour	$250.00	$312.50	$138.89	$13.64	$66.67

FIGURE 4.4
Volume-based overhead allocations by work center after process improvement.

changed? Parts B and C going through the same sequence of work centers now have significantly different costs—based on the higher overhead allocation assigned to them in machining and welding—even when the process and associated costs have not changed at all. What might be inferred regarding the integrity of margin and pricing data derived from these numbers?

If we continued with the example and included not only the complexity of multiple processes and work centers, but also the impact of custom products in thousands of configurations and a nonrepetitive manufacturing environment, the odds of a consistent and accurate allocation of costs on a product basis are about as good as winning the lottery. The reality is that once any variable in the model used to build the overhead rate changes, other costs can be impacted in unpredictable and illogical ways.

The only real guarantee in a low-volume, high-mix environment is that if you get it right in any one month, the same allocation method will not work in the next month due to changes in the mix of products, machines, and work centers. This results is an unending and impossible attempt to spread costs in a predictable way across products in unpredictable mixes and volumes.

Because overhead costs are generally allocated based on units, whether that unit be direct labor hours or machine hours, rather than over total lead time, improvements that reduce lead time often show costs to be increasing, rather than decreasing. The following example illustrates how product costing can actively work against lead time and velocity.

Assume that we have a part that currently goes through four departmental processes in lots of 3000 pieces. The part takes 4 min to lathe, 1 min to drill, 6 min to grind, and 4 min to inspect and pack for a total of 15 min. The drill operation goes through an expensive high-speed drill that is shared by multiple parts with an average wait time for the drill of two days. Labor is valued at $20 per hour and overhead is allocated at a rate of $60 per hour.

Figure 4.5 shows the cost, lead time, and inventory value of the lot:

Lot size = 3,000 / Lead time = 35.4 d	Minutes /part	Minutes /lot	Hour/ lot	Labor/ part at $20/h	Overhead/ part at $60/h	Material/ part ($)	Total inventory value ($)
Lathe	4	12,000	200	$1.33	$4.00		
Wait for drill	2	6,000	100	–	–		
Drill	1	3,000	50	$0.33	$1.00		
Grind	6	18,000	300	$2.00	$6.00		
Inspect and pack	4	12,000	200	$1.33	$4.00		
Total lead time	17	51,000	850	$5.00	$15.00	$10.00	$30.00
Inventory value				$15,000	$45,000	$30,000	$90,000

FIGURE 4.5
Example of a departmental organization before lead time reduction.

Lot size = 300 / Lead time = 3.75 d	Minutes /part	Minutes /lot	Hour/ lot	Labor/ part at $20/h	Overhead/ part at $60/h	Material/ part ($)	Total inventory value ($)
Lathe	4	1,200	20	$1.33	$4.00		
Wait for drill	0	–	–	–	–		
Drill	4	1,200	20	$1.33	$4.00		
Grind	6	1,800	30	$2.00	$6.00		
Inspect and pack	4	1,200	20	$1.33	$4.00		
Total lead time	18	5,400	90	$6.00	$18.00	$10.00	$34.00
Inventory value				$1,800	$5,400	$3,000	$10,200

FIGURE 4.6
Example of a cellular structure after lead time reduction.

The part cost is $30.00 each, which is made up of $5.00 in labor, $15.00 in overhead, and $10.00 in material. (*Note that although the wait time consumes two days of lead time and WIP, it carries no cost.*) It takes 35.4 days for the lot to get through all of the processes. Work in process ranges from $30,000 (material only) to the total value of $90,000, averaging $60,000 in work in process over the total production time.

Now assume that a work cell is formed to process this part. The cell is able to move an existing lathe and grinder to the cell. However, the cost of the high-speed drill is prohibitive. The team determines that a low-cost drill is available, but it will take four times as long to perform the drilling operation. The team also determines that the customer will happily accept lots of 300 in shorter intervals rather than waiting 35 days for the lot of 3000. Figure 4.6 shows the cost, lead time, and inventory value of the lot.

Additional labor is incurred during the drilling operation, adding $1.00 per unit to the part. The additional time on the drill adds another $3.00 per unit to the part for overhead. The resulting product cost of $34.00 ($6.00 in labor, $18.00 in overhead, and $10.00 in material) is higher than the cost of the previous process by $4.00 per unit.

The accounting staff wants to pull the cell apart and go back to functional departments because product costs are going up. However, did they really? Consider the following:

- Customer responsiveness has greatly improved, with lead time reduced by over 30 days!

- Average work in process is significantly improved, going from an overage of $60,000 to an average of only $10,000.
- Even though parts take much longer on the lower speed drill—which is the source of the additional overhead allocation of $3.00 per part—prior to the change the parts were waiting two days to get access to the drill. The additional drill time really has no impact on overall lead time of the part. However, since no overhead is allocated to *wait time,* it appears as though costs are increasing.

To this point, overhead has been discussed in general terms. Cost systems may distinguish *variable* overhead from *fixed* overhead. Variable manufacturing overhead are those costs that will increase in total as output increases. Examples include the cost of electricity to run machines, material handling, and manufacturing supplies. Fixed overhead refers to costs that remain relatively the same over wide ranges of output, that is, depreciation, rent, and salaries of production managers and supervisors.

Whether fixed or variable, the selection of a cost allocation base (or bases) is required to calculate a unit cost. Because variable manufacturing costs fluctuate with production, the assumption is made that the allocation to products of variable overhead is more accurate or reliable than the allocation of fixed overhead. Consider for example, material handling. While this may vary with how much you make, it also varies with mix, schedules, resource availability, and a myriad of other factors. When you operate in a high-mix environment with a wide variety of raw materials, how do you begin to define a cost allocation base for material handling that works from month to month and product to product?

The following chart shows the calculation of an overhead rate of $3.00 to be applied to products for every hour of direct labor, a very common basis for allocating overhead to products in manufacturing companies. The example shows the *variable* portion of the overhead at $2.00 per hour ($20,000/10,000 h) with the assumption that it will go up or down based on direct labor hours as shown. The fixed portion of the overhead is $15,000 regardless of direct labor hours. The rate of $1.50 per direct labor hour is calculated by taking the fixed overhead of $15,000 over the expected, or most likely, number of direct labor hours of 10,000. This results in a combined overhead rate of $3.50 per hour. Therefore, if a product is expected to use 10 h of direct labor, it will be assigned $35 (10 * $3.50) of overhead in its product cost (Figure 4.7).

Does it make sense that the amount of material handling (considered a variable overhead expense in this example) will vary based on the amount of direct labor hours in the department? Does material handling at your facility vary directly with the number of hours your employees work? Is there logic that says with any degree of assurance that your operating supply costs will vary directly with the number of hours your employees work? If your department made the same thing every day, then the correlation might be accurate. However, product mix, variation, and customization options will cause wide differences in the actual overhead per direct labor hour at any time.

The denominator, or allocation base, for the purpose of allocating fixed overhead to obtain a single product cost for use in valuing inventory, is problematic. My college textbook, *Cost Accounting: A Managerial Emphasis*, states: "The selection of an appropriate denominator for the

S&S manufacturing			
Standard direct-labor hours	9,000	10,000	11,000
Variable overhead:			
Material handling	$6,300	$7,000	$6,300
Utilities	9,000	10,000	9,000
Supplies	2,700	3,000	2,700
Total	$18,000	$20,000	$18,000
Variable rate per hour	$2.00	$2.00	$2.00
Fixed overhead:			
Supervision	$3,500	$3,500	$3,500
Depreciation	4,000	4,000	4,000
Rent	5,000	5,000	5,000
Insurance	2,500	2,500	2,500
Total	$15,000	$15,000	$15,000
Fixed rate per hour	$1.50	$1.50	$1.50
Total overhead rate per hour	$3.50	$3.50	$3.50

FIGURE 4.7
Volume-based overhead allocation using direct labor hours.

pre-determination of fixed-overhead rates is a matter of judgment; a dozen independent accountants or engineers would probably decide on a dozen different denominator levels based on the same set of available facts. Thus, the standard product cost would differ, depending on who sets the rate for fixed overhead" (Horngren, 1977). Although this comes from an old edition of the textbook, the statement still rings true. Having said this, what is the integrity and accuracy of this data for the purposes for which it is commonly used?

> **Fully Absorbed Product Cost as a Decision Making Tool**
>
> If 12 different accountants will come up with 12 different answers, how reliable (or useful) is this data for decision making? How accurate, or representative of reality, is it?

The author of the text notes that "Managers should always be careful to distinguish the true behavior of fixed costs from the manner in which fixed costs are assigned to products. In particular, while fixed costs are unitized and allocated for inventory costing purposes in a certain way…managers should be wary of using the same unitized fixed overhead costs for planning and control purposes" (Horngren, 2012). Unfortunately, even though the warning label has been applied to the bottle, fully absorbed product costs—including fixed costs—are used on a daily basis for planning and control purposes in companies all across the country.

Therefore, if fully absorbed costs are misleading for planning and control purposes, and the primary reason for unitizing fixed costs is for the purpose of valuing inventory, then the next logical question is whether we must unitize fixed costs in order to value inventory. What if we unitized *only* the variable components of cost and recorded the fixed portion of the cost as a lump sum rather than attempting to allocate it to products? This eliminates the problem of nonaccountants making incorrect decisions by using fully absorbed product costs, while at the same time meeting the requirement for absorbing fixed costs for inventory valuation. Further detail on this approach can be found in Chapter 11.

4.3 STANDARD COST

 Standard Cost

An estimated or predetermined cost of performing an operation or producing a good or service, under normal conditions.

Standard costs are used as target costs (or basis for comparison with the actual costs) and are developed from historical data analysis or from time and motion studies. They almost always vary from actual costs, because every situation has its share of unpredictable factors.

4.3.1 History and Theory

Standard costing is a costing system that (a) traces direct costs to output produced by multiplying the standard prices or rates by the standard quantities of inputs allowed for actual outputs produced and (b) allocates overhead costs on the basis of the standard overhead cost rates times the standard quantities of the allocations bases allowed for the actual outputs produced.

Horngren, 2012

(Are you confused yet?) Standard costing has its foundations in the industrial revolution and the advent of mass production based on economies of scale. Mass production as illustrated by the assembly line model is represented by the following characteristics:

- Repetitive tasks
- Homogeneous output
- Sequential organization of processes
- Specialized labor

In this environment, the use of predetermined, norm-based standard costs was promoted as the means to control operations and reduce waste. The comparison of actual cost to these norms results in variances. Variances from norms are opportunities for improvement or the opportunity to bring a cost back in line with the *norm*.

The production volume variance, also known as the denominator variance, is an example from standard costing that illustrates the motivation to *make more*. A favorable denominator variance arises when you operate at or above the activity level selected as the denominator for computing the product-costing rate. An unfavorable denominator variance arises when you operate at less than the selected activity level. While caution should be used in drawing conclusions based on these variances (whether favorable or unfavorable), and cost accounting books do indeed include cautionary warnings to this effect, they still carry the label *favorable* and *unfavorable*. They move in a *favorable* direction when you fill capacity, without respect to demand.

Therefore, when your denominator is direct labor hours, there is an assumed benefit to consume *more* direct labor hours to spread overhead costs over more units. When your denominator is machine hours, there is an assumed benefit to consume *more* machine hours to spread overhead cost over more units.

4.3.2 Why Standard Cost Variance Analysis Is Not Value-Added Work

Under standard costing, any differences between standard cost (standard unit costs × actual units produced) and actual cost as recorded by the accounting system are charged to variance accounts. Variance accounts are then analyzed to determine what caused the discrepancy between the normalized (standard) cost and actual cost. Variance accounts are defined for material variances, labor variances, and overhead variances. Each variance can further be segregated between price variances (components cost more or less than standard) and efficiency variances (usage is more or less than standard).

Variances include the following:

- Material price variances
- Material efficiency variances
- Direct labor price variances
- Direct labor efficiency variances
- Variable overhead efficiency variances
- Variable overhead spending variances

- Fixed overhead cost variances
- Production volume variances

Standard cost advocates point out that variances can point out process issues and lead to continuous improvement efforts. And while this may be true in some manufacturing environments, it is also true that the discipline, care, feeding, and maintenance required for any transaction-intensive standard cost system are substantial. Lean accounting advocates would point out that there are simpler, easier, and often more accurate methods to attain the same result.

When a manufacturer makes a limited number of parts, using a limited number of raw materials in a fixed sequence of steps, it might be a reasonable task to analyze variances and determine the exact source of the discrepancy.

Statistically, if a manufacturer has 1000 end items, each of which uses an average of 10 raw materials, and goes through an average of 10 processing steps, the source of an efficiency variance could be in any of $1,000 \times 10 \times 10 = 100,000$ places to look!

In my experience with standard cost, the root cause of a variance is just as likely to be a procedural accounting issue as a process (manufacturing) issue. Revisions to bills of material, products that are produced before cost has been updated, missing standard costs, improper assignments of General Ledger codes, improper treatment of returns (vendor or customer), timing or cutoff issues, backdating and improper backdating of transactions—all cause variances. It takes an enormous amount of detective work and *time* to scour through transactions, reports, and process costing entries and uncover these discrepancies. Although it may feel like a success when you get there (aha! I found it!), you need to ask yourself if by uncovering the source of the variance—did you add any value? Will the company make any more money? Has the process been improved? If the answer is no, then think about what type of activities might have been a more productive use of your time.

The other common experience with standard cost is that operations personnel universally distrust the numbers. And why not? Operations personnel are the most aware of the deficiencies or inaccuracies of the standards based on their knowledge of daily operations. They are also often perplexed when presented with financial statements that display data in complex variance formats that mask the total cost of material or labor by dividing it into multiple variances. They are also frustrated by timeliness, or lack thereof, of the information. What is the point of pointing out a variance that occurred as long as five weeks ago (with a monthly reporting cycle and one week to close the books)? If, for example, you have unearthed a material usage variance that is related to scrap, is not the proper time to deal with that when it occurs? How useful is this information when the process is no longer running (and, in a high-mix business, may not run again for months)? When variances are viewed by management as indication of operations effectiveness, does management know and fully understand how the standard was set against which the variance was reported? Does management understand how the complex interaction of mix, people, and machines impacts the variance?

When analyzing variances, the assumption is made that if the variance was eliminated, the difference would drop right to the bottom line. This is simply not the case. Businesses are systems with interrelated processes and complex dynamics. Eliminating one variance may in fact result in higher inventory and/or higher costs in other areas. Isolated unfavorable variances and/or specific product cost increases are often the reason why projects that actually reduce lead time and inventory are discontinued. And this is how your cost system may be making your customer wait (Figure 4.8).

Measurement	Behavior	Results
Purchase price variance	Negotiate based on quantity breaks	Excess inventory and carrying costs
Machine utilization	Run excess over required to maximize utilization	Excess inventory and the wrong inventory
Setup built into standards	Encourages high run quantities	Excess inventory
Scrap factor built into standard	No action if no variance	Inflated standard, no improvement

FIGURE 4.8
What you measure matters!

SCRAP IN STANDARDS

Have you heard this one before? "It's okay because we have 4% scrap built into the price."

Just because it is built into the standard cost, and price, does not make it okay. Every opportunity to reduce scrap (whether the rate is above or below standard) is an opportunity to save material, and even more importantly—time.

Does anyone know when the last time the scrap factors were updated? How confident are you that the current standards are accurate and represent a *standard* or *normal* amount of scrap?

Scrap is a double whammy. You have to make enough parts to replace the scrap, so you consume twice the material and twice the time. In the meantime, you could have been making other sellable parts to turn into cash.

If your scrap reports show the variance from standard, consider what they are telling you. Should you celebrate a positive variance? Hurrah! We only spent $10,000 and 100 h when our standards say we should have $15,000 in scrap that consumed 150 h! The better way to look at this is the $10,000 and 100 h opportunity that lies in front of you rather than the $5,000 positive variance.

Measure improvements over time, in both dollars and time saved. This will tell you much more than comparing scrap to an arbitrary standard.

4.4 ACTIVITY-BASED COSTING: IS IT REALLY AS EASY AS ABC?

4.4.1 Cost Drivers: The Solution?

ABC attempts to address the concern of distortion and improper allocation of overhead created by oversimplified allocations using just one variable—machine hours or labor hours. ABC creates multiple allocation methods based on *cost drivers*. In order to apply ABC, one must figure which activities are used by each product, how much of the activity applies to the product, and what each activity costs. Rather than applying a general overhead rate, say $50 per hour, to encompass indirect expenses (rent, depreciation, indirect labor/supervision, and operating supplies)—a separate rate and allocation base will be developed for each line item based on its *cost driver.*

For example, the rent line item would be allocated to work centers based on square footage, which would be the cost driver for this line item at the work center. If the rent is $10,000 per month, the relative square footage of each work center would determine the work center allocation (Figure 4.9).

Knowing this, the next step is to determine how much of work center allocation to give to each unit. In other words, what is the best unit to use to describe how the activity (rent) is consumed by resources (products)? Assume we decide to allocate the work center rate based on the number of hours in each work center, we can now determine the cost driver rate per unit (Figure 4.10).

The cost per product for *rent* can now be determined by accumulating the unit costs for each work center the product goes through as follows (Figure 4.11).

We have now successfully determined the activity-based cost by item for rent. The sum of the items (with minor rounding) comes out to the $10,000 per month cost.

Keeping in mind that we just went through *one* line item (*rent*) and *three* products, imagine the computations required for a complex mix of work centers, activities, and parts. Even after all the work, at the end of the day, the choice of the activities and cost drivers determines the cost. The cost is

$10,000 rent to be allocated	Machining	Welding	Heat treat	Assembly	Total
Square footage	50,000	25,000	5,000	20,000	100,000
% of total	50%	25%	5%	20%	100%
Rent $ (activity cost)	$5,000	$2,500	$500	$2,000	$10,000

FIGURE 4.9
ABC cost driver allocation.

	Machining	Welding	Heat treat	Assembly	Total
Rent $ (activity cost)	$5,000	$2,500	$500	$2,000	$10,000
Total hours	14,000	8,000	18,000	110,000	150,000
Cost/hour	$0.357	$0.313	$0.028	$0.018	$0.0667

FIGURE 4.10
ABC cost driver rates.

$10,000 to be allocated	Machining	Welding	Heat treat	Assembly	Total rent
Product A				50000 × $0.018	$900
Product B	6000 × $0.357		6000 × $0.028	48000 × $0.018	$3,174
Product C	8000 × $0.357	8000 × $0.313	12000 × $0.028	12000 × $0.018	$5,912
Total rent					$9,986

FIGURE 4.11
ABC unit cost.

still determined based on allocations which are based on the assumption that indirect costs can somehow *attach* themselves to a part in a fashion that represents an accurate cost.

4.4.2 Theory and Practice

Although the concept of ABC systems is widely disseminated, and discussed in cost accounting courses, there is limited evidence of the use of ABC by firms, documented in surveys such as those by Innes and Mitchell (1995, 2000). One reason is the absolute complexity and transactional burden imposed by such a system. A study published by the American Accounting Association reports a large financial services firm employs 14 persons to maintain its ABC system; and another that reported processing of cost reports took 3 days for 150 activities, 10,000 orders, and 45,000 line items (Balakrishnan et al., 2012b).

H. Thomas Johnson, as published in *Management Accounting*, says that to change conventional cost accounting to ABC is like *rearranging deck chairs on the Titanic.* Johnson goes on to say, "the pathway to global competitive excellence is not reached by doing better what should not be done at all" (Johnson, 1992, p. 30). Even though an attempt is made to legitimize allocations by using cost drivers, the end result is still that overhead costs are stocked in products, which motivates inventory buildup by increasing bottom-line income when inventory is growing. In fact, the selection of drivers remains somewhat subjective and the rates for the drivers still depend on static data which do not allow for the dynamics that variability in mix, throughput, and utilization can have on the rates. The crux of the issue is not really whether we use labor or machines hours as an allocation base, or whether we use one or many cost drivers—the issue is the allocation of costs to products. *The variability of production mix and volume makes any and all allocation methods invalid.*

4.5 LEAN ACCOUNTING AND VALUE STREAMS

Lean manufacturing is a business management tool that focuses on reducing waste from production processes. The most significant source of waste is overproduction.

> Overproduction causes all kinds of waste, not just excess inventory and money tied up in that inventory. Batches of parts must be stored, requiring storage space; handled, requiring people and equipment; sorted; and reworked. Overproduction results in shortages, because people are busy making the wrong things. It means you need extra operators and equipment capacity, because you are using some of your labor and equipment to produce parts that are not yet needed. It also lengthens the lead time, which impairs your flexibility to respond to customer requirements. The constant attention Toyota puts on avoiding overproduction is what most clearly distinguishes their value streams from mass production streams. Mass production thinking says that the more and faster you produce, the cheaper it is to produce. But this is true only from a direct-cost-per-item perspective as measured by traditional accounting practices, and ignores all the other very real costs associated with overproduction and the wastes it causes.

Rother and Shook, 2009

Since traditional accounting practices do not consider overproduction, wastes, or time—it stands to reason that new accounting practices and financial presentations should be developed. Lean accounting is an offshoot of Lean manufacturing that seeks to eliminate waste from a company's resources by applying Lean manufacturing principles to the company's financial functions. Lean accounting favors elimination of fully absorbed product cost because it:

- Requires overhead allocations that motivate nonlean behavior (make more to spread cost over more, put inventory on shelf)
- Leads to poor decisions for make vs. buy vs. outsource, new equipment, and pricing

Furthermore, Lean accounting favors the elimination of standard cost because it requires transaction-intensive work with detailed reporting of variances that is non-value added work.

Lean accounting replaces standard cost and full absorption cost systems with value stream costing. A value stream consists of all the processes required to create value for the customer, organized as a team accountable for increasing value and profitability through continuous improvement. A value stream is never one department or work center or grouping of like machines; it is generally associated with cellular manufacturing designed to produce a product from start to finish in the cell. In value stream costing, all costs that are directly attributable to the value stream are recorded in value stream accounts with little or no allocation. Value stream costing operates on the assumption that the absorption of costs that occur outside the value stream does not provide any useful information for managing or improving value stream processes. Value stream costing does not collect costs by job or product. The costs are collected in total and the value stream manager (or cell itself) has P&L responsibility for the value stream. Proponents of value stream costing cite that cost will vary based on mix, so if any product can have different costs at any point in time, why worry about it? They say you can figure out what it takes to run a value stream, but not what it costs to run a product. Instead, scorecards for the value stream report average cost per unit across all products. Herein lies the primary objection to Lean Accounting. Management accounting systems were designed to facilitate efforts to control costs, measure and improve productivity, and report accurate costs for make/buy and pricing decisions. In a custom manufacturing environment, even in a cell with similar products, there is often wide variation in run times, material requirements, operator requirements, and machines utilized. In this case, *average unit cost* does not tell anyone much about how effective the cell was. Issues raised with respect to value stream accounting in a custom environment revolve around the fact that it does not compute product costs:

- What kind of guidance does the cell have at a job level to know when things are not right and raise the flag if there are no targets?
- If the job does not go as quoted, how will this be spotted and addressed?
- Flow rates are not uniform and the rate and mix of demand are out of the control of the cell. Therefore, results can fluctuate widely and there is no measure to compare expected to actual results.

4.5.1 Toyota Production System (TPS)

Taiichi Ohno is considered to be the father of the TPS which was the foundation of Lean Manufacturing in the United States. He wrote several books about the system, including *Toyota Production System: Beyond*

Large-Scale Production. A couple of quotes from Taiichi Ohno encapsulate the thinking that underlies the TPS:

> All we are doing is looking at the time line, from the moment the customer gives us an order to the point where we collect the cash. And we are reducing the time line by reducing the non-value adding wastes.

> Costs do not exist to be calculated. Costs exist to be reduced.

Taiichi Ohno

In other words, reducing lead time has the potential to increase volume with the same (or lower) fixed costs. While U.S. manufacturers focused on waste, flow, and takt time—they ignored the very important components of velocity and lead time. One might say that the Lean movement in the United States has often focused on the trees (waste) rather than on the forest (time from order to cash). A colleague of mine refers to *Big Picture Lean,* which refers to selecting waste elimination projects in context of their impact on lead time reduction.

4.5.2 Focus on Time Line Reduction

As illustrated earlier when discussing the concepts of Quick Response Manufacturing, focusing on the gray space (which can be further defined in an accounting context as the variable costs associated with a product) will not significantly reduce lead time or costs when costs are defined in a system-wide or value stream context. However, when we focus on velocity and lead time reduction, the impact on the bottom line is significant. If our products contribute an average of $5.00 for every day of lead time, and we are now able to ship more products by eliminating waste (in the form of downtime, scrap, setup reduction) we have increased our contribution. If we are able to ship the same amount of products in less time (reduced lead time), we have also increased our contribution. If we are able to do *both*, that is, ship more in shorter time, our contribution multiplies. This requires *focused* rather than random waste elimination. If the elimination of waste is focused first and foremost on waste that will result in a reduction of lead time, the opportunity for increased velocity exists.

Lead time reduction, and velocity, comes in three forms:

1. *Elimination of wait time and queues.* Activities in this category include lot size reduction, cellular structure, and cross-training. These activities will result in reduced lead time but may also translate to increased costs when calculated in a traditional fashion.

2. White space reduction activities that result in *cost reduction.* Examples associated with inventory reduction include lower carrying cost, lower inventory obsolescence, reduction of handling costs, lower counting costs, and reduction of transaction costs. However, rarely is the cost associated with consuming resources that could have been used to make something that could ship to a customer considered. These costs include the time spent expediting, planning, and rescheduling that comes with making the *wrong* things.
3. White space reduction activities that result in *additional capacity.* Examples include setup reduction, scrap or rework reduction, make to order vs. make to stock, preventive maintenance to reduce downtime, optimizing flow (eliminating steps, combining steps, or changing routings), and reducing travel time with point of use supplies and materials.

Financial justifications typically focus only on activities in the second category, where *hard dollars* can be demonstrated. Customer responsiveness has a market value and offers competitive advantage. Spare capacity has a value both in terms of avoiding the queues that are created when resources are overutilized, but also in the form of incremental sales potential. Critics may point out that this assumes that sales are there for the taking, providing unlimited work to the cell. Consider this: If your business was able to offer products at a fraction of the lead time of your competitors, for the same price, what would be the impact on your sales? One company cites the following "...the ability to take advantage of incremental demand by executing the additional sales opportunities. In a seasonal business with a three month window, our average supplier lead-time was also about three months. In other words, we had *no* ability to adjust our schedules to react to demand. Over seven years we worked with our suppliers to lower their lead time to an average of just over two weeks. After that, we were very successful in not only changing mix but also raising (or lowering) overall volumes to match demand with the sales season. This helped us avoid having product that wouldn't sell (at a cost) and also put us in a position to book 'incremental' profits."*

---

* Paul D. Ericksen, President and Chief Executive Officer, Build to Demand Inc.

4.6 THEORY OF CONSTRAINTS
AND THROUGHPUT ACCOUNTING

Throughput Accounting (TA) is a principle-based and simplified manage-ment accounting approach that provides managers with decision support information for enterprise profitability improvement. TA was proposed by Thomas Corbett as an alternative to traditional cost accounting when applying Theory of Constraints, as developed by Eliyahu M. Goldratt. As such, Throughput Accounting is not a product costing methodology. It is cash focused and does not allocate overhead costs to products and services sold or provided by an enterprise. Considering the laws of variation, only costs that vary totally with units of output, for example, raw materials, are allocated to products and services which are deducted from sales to determine throughput.

Some definitions for acronyms used in TA are as follows:

Totally Variable Cost (TVC) stands for the cost that varies directly with production volume. If the company produces and sells another unit of the product it will incur this amount, and if it produces one unit less it will not incur this cost. The clearest example is material cost and most purists include only material costs in TVC.
Capacity Constraint Resource (CCR) is the resource that limits capacity, the weakest link.
Throughput per Unit (Tu) = Price per Unit –TVC per Unit.

Putting this together, a product's throughput is calculated as shown in Figure 4.12.

A	B	C	D (B-C)	E	F (D/E)
Product	Price/unit	TVC/unit	Throughput/unit (Tu)	Time on CCR	Throughput/time on CCR
A	$50	$35	$15	1	$15.00
B	$75	$50	$25	10	$2.50
C	$100	$65	$35	5	$7.00

FIGURE 4.12
Throughput accounting. (From Corbett, T., *Throughput Accounting.* The North River Press, Great Barrington, MA, 1998. With permission.)

This is quite different from Lean accounting, where the idea of product cost is disregarded in favor of value stream contribution. This analysis shows thatProduct A, even though it has the lowest contribution based on price (30% or $15 Tu/$50 Price) generates the most contribution per time on the CCR. This is proposed as an alternative to standard costing for making determinations of price and make/buy decisions because it includes variable cost only (no overheads) *and* because it includes the concept of time.

The advantages to throughput accounting are that it looks at variable cost and overcomes the problem of overhead absorption. It provides product contribution information, and it incorporates the concept of time (in the form of production time or gray space).

The disadvantages to throughput accounting are that it does not offer a good solution to the GAAP requirement for full absorption of overheads, as it ignores overhead. Additionally, the concept of the CCR is difficult in some environments; in particular, low-volume, high-mix environments where the constraint is constantly changing.

4.7 TIME-BASED ACCOUNTING (TBA)

Following the publication of *Competing Against Time* (Stalk and Hout, 1990) some proposals were presented for *Time-Based Accounting*. The proposals focused on how to use time to allocate overheads to incorporate the concept of time. Time-Driven Activity-Based Costing (TDABC) as introduced by Robert Kaplan in 2004 delinks supply and use of resources with the use of time equations to determine the quantity of resources consumed by a cost object. TDABC requires estimates of only two parameters:

1. The unit cost of supplying capacity
2. The time required to perform a transaction or an activity

Another time-based model uses cycle time or machine hours to allocate overhead, which is a fairly common allocation basis option along with direct labor hours or dollars.

4.8 ABSORBING COSTS ON A MACRO LEVEL ELIMINATES ALLOCATIONS

The attempt to find some meaningful way to allocate overhead is a general response to GAAP requirements for full absorption. Because of our bias to total product costs and full absorption, we assume that it is necessary to calculate overhead, and total cost, at a product level. In fact, GAAP requires no such thing. *It is possible to absorb overhead into your inventory in one entry (or pool), rather than attempting to allocate it among all products.* This is acceptable and meets all GAAP requirements. Therefore, the attempts to allocate on a product basis simply come down to trying to perfect something that should not be done in the first place! Someone once told me that a computer makes it possible to do the wrong thing many times faster. Just because technology enables complex allocation methods and formulas to allocate overhead over many items in a short time does not make it the right thing to do. Just because your ERP system includes a standard cost module does not make standard cost the best way to look at your product costs, nor does it make the costs accurate for decision making and profitability analysis.

5

What Does GAAP Have to Do with It?

 Definition of "GAAP"

Generally accepted accounting principles: A widely accepted set of rules, conventions, standards, and procedures for reporting financial information, as established by the Financial Accounting Standards Board (FASB).

Most companies in the United States adhere to GAAP to maintain consistency and comparability in the reporting of financial information. If GAAP did not exist, there would be little to no assurance to investors, creditors, and stakeholders of a company that financial statements are a fair, accurate, and consistent representation of operations. Finally, without GAAP, investors could not compare the results of one potential investment against another—as they could have been prepared under different accounting methods, treatments, and assumptions.

GAAP is not required by law, but not adhering to GAAP has severe consequences, both from an audit and tax standpoint. The U.S. Securities and Exchange Commission (SEC) requires publicly traded companies and other regulated companies to follow GAAP for financial reporting. Public accounting firms that review financial records and statements issue an opinion as to whether the statements are a true and fair representation of financial condition. A clean, or unqualified opinion, includes an assessment that the financial statements have been prepared using GAAP, which have been consistently applied. Therefore, accountants or financial analysts involved in the financial reporting of a company will need to understand and enforce the principles of GAAP; this helps set the standard for the organization and reduces the risk of tax problems and erroneous reporting of transactions across all departments.

5.1 WHAT GAAP REALLY REQUIRES (AND IT'S NOT STANDARD COST)

> Businesses can use any rational and systematic method to assign costs to the inventory sold during the accounting period.

GAAP is based on the following key accounting principles:

The *revenue recognition principle* states that, under the accrual basis of accounting, revenue is recorded only when an entity has substantially completed a revenue generation process; thus, you record revenue when it has been earned.

In accrual accounting, the *matching principle* states that expenses should be recorded during the period in which they are incurred, regardless of when the transfer of cash occurs.

Therefore, under GAAP, the expenses associated with creating a product that is unsold cannot be recorded until the sale occurs; that is, the expenses must be *matched* to the sale. Therefore, these principles are the origin of inventory as a way to account for unsold product, and the ensuing need to value the costs associated with that same inventory. As inventory is produced, costs are associated with that production and are absorbed into inventory. Therefore, if your inventory goes up, some of the expenses that have been incurred in the period are absorbed into inventory, which increases profits for the period. When the inventory is sold, the costs associated with the inventory are recorded as expenses at the time of sale. Therefore, when your inventory goes down, the expenses associated with the sell down of inventory are recorded and result in a reduction of period profits. The capitalization of manufacturing costs into inventory impacts profit and loss and creates potential for overstatement and understatement of profits. The more inventory you have, the greater the potential for error.

The longer you keep inventory, and if your rate of production is not the same as the rate that product ships, the potential for error is even greater. Practices that reduce lead time and match production to demand help reduce the potential for these type of misstatements.

GAAP requires absorption costing because both variable and fixed costs are required to produce goods, and both types of costs should be reflected in inventory, regardless of their differences in behavior patterns. In practice, absorption costing is far from uniform in its application. There are many different inventory methods (first-in, first-out; last-in, first-out, weighted average, specific identification—to name a few). As we have seen, there are also many different assumptions for overhead allocation, including direct labor hours, machine hours, cycle times, and volume.

It is generally agreed, even by proponents of absorption costing, that variable (or direct) cost approaches provide better information for managerial decisions. This is contrasted with the theory that full absorption costing is most accurate for inventory valuation and cost of goods sold. In practice, faced with the time and effort required to maintain *two* accounting systems—both direct and absorption—firms choose to maintain the one that is required by GAAP.

However, GAAP does not dictate the method of assigning costs to inventory. Businesses can use any rational and systematic method to assign costs to inventory sold during an accounting period. GAAP does not even dictate individual *product* costs, and it certainly does not require standard cost. It is not difficult to estimate the total amount of overhead in your inventory, simply by calculating overhead per day and multiplying by the days on hand. For example, if you incur $30,000 of overhead per month, this is $1,000 per day. If you carry 20 days of inventory, this amounts to $20,000 of overhead to be recorded in the inventory. This can be booked with one journal entry for the change from the prior month. When making a monthly adjustment, the method is best applied when days on hand are less than 1 month. In this case, it is easy to associate the costs for the month with the product in inventory. To make the calculation, the timing of the closing process comes into play. Cost of sales, used to calculate days in inventory may not be known until the inventory entries have been booked (absorbed into inventory). However, *days of direct costs in inventory* can be calculated with the following information:

- *Direct costs in beginning inventory*: The last period's closing inventory before booking overhead adjustment. It includes both WIP and finished goods in this calculation, for days of stock, whether partially or fully complete, on hand.

- *Direct costs in ending inventory*: This period's inventory before booking overhead adjustment. Again, includes WIP and finished goods.
- *Direct cost of sales*: cost of sales before overhead adjustment, but after inventory adjustment for direct costs.
- *Overhead*: if the entry is to be booked before the final numbers for the current month fixed costs are available, and if overhead does not fluctuate significantly month to month, use an average (e.g., a rolling 3-month average).

Since overhead is booked with one macro entry, these entries are easily isolated which makes this data readily available. Eliminating the overhead portion of inventory and costs of sales put them on a direct cost basis. For example, for an average inventory with $100,000 in direct cost, and direct cost of sales is $500,000; the inventory is turning five times. If the period being analyzed is a month, this means that the days on hand are 30/5 = 6. An example of how this works from month to month is shown in Figure 5.1.

The end result is no different from assigning overhead to products; you just record the total dollar value rather than attempting to allocate it on a product-by-product basis. This avoids the pitfalls of using fully absorbed product costs for decision making. You can use this formula to adjust your inventory to *GAAP* when necessary. For publicly held companies, this will be on a monthly basis. For privately held companies, overhead expenses may be recorded as incurred on a monthly basis with an adjustment to a

---

Inventory days = Days in period * average inventory/cost of goods sold (COGS)

Overhead in inventory = Overhead/days in period * Days in inventory

		Month 1	Month 2	Month 3
A	Starting inventory (direct costs)	$500,000	$250,000	$600,000
B	Ending inventory (direct costs)	$250,000	$600,000	$400,000
C	Direct cost of sales (excluding overhead)	$500,000	$300,000	$500,000
D	Days in period	30	30	30
$E = D*((A + B)/2)/C$	Inventory days	22.5	42.5	30.0
F	Overhead dollars	$50,000	$50,000	$50,000
$G = F/D*E$	Overhead in inventory	$37,500	$70,833	$50,000

FIGURE 5.1
Calculating overhead in inventory.

full-absorption basis with one entry at year end. Sample entries and calculations are included in Chapter 11.

The treatment of WIP, as noted above, depends on how the company values WIP in the first place. Methods vary from not valuing it at all, to the other end of the spectrum with full product costing for WIP. If you practice Lean and/or lead time reduction strategies, your WIP will be minimized and may be immaterial. In this case, you may not value your WIP at all, other than perhaps at year end. Other companies change product identities at each stage of the process, and carry cost information for intermediate products. In this case, the treatment is as described earlier, that is, use the direct cost portion of the value and combine WIP with finished goods. Some companies, especially those with one-of-a-kind custom products, accumulate costs as they go. This is referred to as *job costing*. These costs carry with the work order. In this case, use the accumulated direct costs of the work in process. Finally, some companies use percentage of completion to estimate WIP, by applying the estimated percent complete to the final cost. In this case, apply the percentage complete to the direct cost portion of the final cost to the overhead to determine the portion to record in inventory.

6

Variation, or Stuff Happens

A colleague of mine recently gave a talk and asked the audience "How many of you have conducted one or more Lean projects in your company?" Virtually every hand in the room went up. Next he asked how many were happy with the results. In response to this question, only one hand went up.

Increasingly, I hear concerns regarding the lack of quantifiable results, or diminishing returns, from Lean initiatives based on waste elimination. Interestingly enough, the micro level (drill-down) focus on individual products and operations may actually be part of the problem. Looking at the process from a macro level that considers the systemic effects of variation can provide insights on which Lean tools can be used and how to focus the use of those tools to produce results.

When viewed from a macro level, we can better see where we should focus our efforts to produce the desired results in the system and achieve the benefits we are looking for. For example, on which machine will setup reduction yield the greatest benefit? What skills should we focus on in cross-training in order to eliminate bottlenecks?

Knowing the critical path is important, as it can help focus continuous improvement initiatives. The critical path can tell you where the greatest opportunities for waste reduction and lead time improvement lie. Focus these activities on operations on the critical path, because saving time in these activities will result in an overall reduction in lead time.

However, honing in on waste without considering the impact that variation has on the entire system may lead you in the wrong direction.

6.1 VARIATION

Variation, or randomness, exists in systems. If you search for the words *variation* or *variability* in this text, you will find over 60 references! Variation plays a huge role in the ability to complete work on time and ultimately on product cost. Variation can come from varying levels of demand, equipment breakdowns, scrap and rework effects, material issues, employees calling in sick, or any of the dozens of reasons that turn operations managers into fire fighters on any given day of the week. Manufacturing plants are the embodiment of organized or disorganized chaos.

For this very reason, Lean initiatives seek to eliminate, or eradicate, variation. If you look at the micro level, that is, one product at one machine, you can reduce variability in the run time per piece. You can reduce the set up times, but there will still be some variation from product to product. Even if variation in run and setup time could be totally eliminated, there will still be randomness in the system which will manifest itself in varying wait times and queues. Lean tools operate on the belief that causes can be determined, and problems can be solved, by deconstructing the problem into smaller and smaller pieces. What if the problem is caused by the relationship between the pieces, rather than within the piece itself?

What about takt time, or the determination of the rate at which the system must operate to match customer demand? Again, on a micro level—or one product at one machine or a predetermined group of machines—the calculation is fairly straightforward. However, add in variability in machine availability, people availability, demand swings, *and* mix variation, and your takt time changes on a daily (or even hourly) basis. Can you calculate takt time at a system level? Certainly not without accounting for variation.

Accounting for the fact that things happen—that randomness cannot be totally eliminated—is not a bad strategy. Building in the correct amount of delay and doing things to strategically mitigate it makes sense. For example, putting extra capacity in the right places to accommodate variation can make a strategic difference in your ability to handle demand variation. The question is how much, and what is the benefit? For example, what decision would you make if you knew that a 5% increase in capacity would result in a 50% improvement in lead time?

6.2 FALLACY OF SCHEDULING MODELS IN ENTERPRISE RESOURCE PLANNING

Have you been stuck in rush hour traffic? If so, you have experienced the reality that waiting, and resultant queues, are exacerbated by high utilization. It is not a difficult concept; when you put more cars on the road than it was designed to handle, there will be lines and waiting.

And yet, every day, we attempt to schedule our plants with no consideration of the impact of utilization. Does your scheduling system add in additional delay time as utilization grows? If not, your schedules are less and less attainable the busier you get.

The real-life examples of how high utilization creates queues can be explained by a branch of mathematics called *queuing theory*. Queuing theory creates mathematical models that explain the phenomenon of the exponential growth of wait time as utilization exceeds a certain level.

6.3 MATHEMATICS CAN PROVIDE USEFUL INSIGHTS

Applied mathematics is the story problem, or the use of mathematics to solve real-life problems. How do we use math to model real-life production story problems? For example, what do we need to change to reduce lead time? What is the best lot size to minimize both lead time and work in process? How many machines should we have? If I add a machine, what will be the impact on lead time? How many people do I need, and what combination of skillsets? If I pay to send an operator to machinist skill, what will be the impact on lead time?

There is a mathematical formula for lead time. If you want to model your operation, you need demand information, job information (set up time and run time), and resource information (number and availability). Up to this point, you have the data and model used by most advanced planning and scheduling (APS) systems.

However, in order to actually model reality, you must recognize that the actual time required on any resource is also impacted by the variability in arrivals *and* job times, and the utilization on the resource. Variation changes everything! You must consider variation to properly assess the correct amount of resources (people and equipment) that will be required to meet lead time objectives.

The mathematical formulas for lead time are further detailed in Chapter 13. Lead time, is after all, simply a sum of job time (set up plus processing time) and average queue (wait) time. The queue time can be calculated if you know the variability and the utilization levels of the resources. Note that queue time can be created by waiting for equipment *or* waiting for labor (operators). High utilization of either type of resource will create wait time.

There is a mathematical, or story problem, explanation of rush hour traffic and lines in the grocery store the day before a holiday. As machines, or people, exceed 75% of capacity, lead time increases exponentially. The job time (set up and process time) is unchanged. What changes is the queue, or wait time. It is worth noting that while most accountants, and many operations managers, would view 100% utilization as *ideal*, in reality achieving that level of utilization will add to lead time and be harmful to your ability to respond to customers.

The conclusion that can be drawn is that any scheduling or rough cut capacity planning system that ignores variability and utilization is flawed and ignores mathematical principles. Does your scheduling system consider variability and utilization when calculating available to promise and shop floor schedules?

6.4 MODELING YOUR VALUE STREAM

Using the value stream modeling technique, we can produce the following graphs and estimates for the utilization of equipment in a cell. The yellow part of the bars shows the time the equipment is waiting for labor and the resulting impact on utilization. Most enterprise resource planning applications report no capacity issues in this situation, because without considering wait time, the resources are under capacity. In reality, two resources—the Mill and the Lathe—are over capacity. Even though they are idle, they cannot process work because they do not have the labor required to do so (Figure 6.1).

Likewise, the lead time for any part can be modeled, but not without considering the impact of variation. What is the variation in the size or time required for jobs? What is the variability in the timing that jobs arrive to be processed? If you are a custom manufacturer, can you eliminate the variation that is inherent to your business model? What is unique about

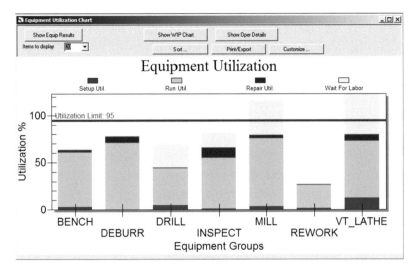

FIGURE 6.1
Utilization with wait for labor. (Reprinted with permission from Build to Demand, Inc., Mountain View, California.)

Figure 6.2 is the incorporation of reality and the effect that the interaction of people and machines has on lead time:

- Wait for labor is shown in yellow.
- Wait for equipment is shown in red.
- Wait for rest of the lot is shown in pink.

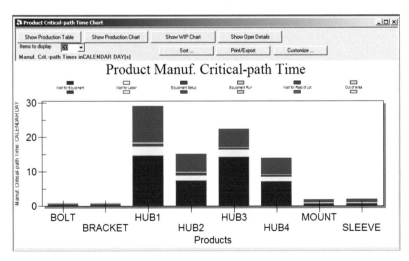

FIGURE 6.2
MCT of products with wait for equipment, labor, and rest of lot. (Reprinted with permission from Build to Demand, Inc., Mountain View, California.)

In point of fact, the lead time for any product as measured by manufacturing critical path time (MCT) depends on the availability of people and machines at *specific* times. Variation must be incorporated to allow for the reality that *stuff happens*. All manufacturers can work to eliminate variation in the form of scrap, rework, equipment downtime, and other factors that can be considered *waste*. Custom and make-to-order manufacturers, however, must consider the variation that is inherent in the business model. The impact of this type of variation needs to be understood and managed for effective lead time reduction. Recognize that the *wait time* (waiting for equipment, waiting for labor, and waiting for the rest of the lot) has a cost, even if traditional cost accounting does not recognize that cost. Product cost calculates the cost incurred during the active processing time, but not the cost that accrues while the product is waiting for resources. Accounting must acknowledge the cost/benefit relationship of allowing for variation in the form of spare capacity and resources.

7

Labor: Direct or Indirect? Cross-Trained or Specialized?

Time and Money and Labor

It is about time to rethink the value of categorizing labor as direct and indirect. Can we learn more about how we are using labor to add value by looking at the labor cost of the cell or value stream rather than looking at the labor cost per unit of product?

Direct labor cost is payroll cost that can be specifically and consistently assigned to or associated with the manufacture of a product. Historically, it was a category used for wages of production line workers. The distinction between direct and indirect labor is an accounting distinction that also has its roots in mass production and the assembly line model. By so distinguishing costs, companies could measure efficiency or productivity of workers by studying how long, on average, it takes a worker to produce one unit, which was categorized as direct labor cost per item. This enabled calculation and reporting of direct labor variances and labor efficiency. The calculation of direct labor cost per unit is fraught with the same absorption and allocation issues as overhead.

1. *Average wage rate and nonproductive time*: In order to come up with a labor cost per unit, we need to know how many units a worker can make in an hour and what the average wage rate is. If a worker can make 100 units in an hour and the average wage is $12 per hour, each unit has a direct labor cost of ($12/100) = $.12. However, how do we account for hours employees classified as direct labor spend in meetings, training, or on vacation—when they are not *directly* involved in the production process? If we do not factor this in, we will be under-absorbed. In other words, when we multiply all of the units made by the direct labor cost and compare to our actual payroll cost, we will come up with a lower number due to *nonproductive* time. To correct for this, and make sure our inventory costs are accurate, we will either adjust the labor rate upwards or the capacity downwards (practical capacity).

2. *Labor efficiency*: Labor efficiency measures motivate the attainment of 100% efficiency as the ideal. 100% efficiency indicates that direct labor personnel are making products at standard rates 100% of the time. The problem is that *nonproductive* time, as defined by cost accounting, can be the most productive time of all! In the 100% efficient world, there would be no training. There would be no continuous improvement project work. There would also be a backlog and lead time issues. If you want to keep everyone busy all the time, you will either create a backlog or you will build inventory. Because demand is never level, particularly in a make-to-order environment, in periods of peak demand you will not be able to keep up and you will create a backlog—or create overtime. During slow periods, if you keep everyone busy you will create inventory. Unless you have the option to add and subtract labor to exactly match demand, you cannot achieve 100% efficiency. Because of the skills required for custom manufacturing, having skilled labor available to *come and go as needed* is rarely an option. Being a responsible employer and an employer of choice requires some stability for employees in terms of hours and job security. Therefore, when production volumes go up and down, direct labor rarely fluctuates by the same percentage in a direct relationship to production hours. In reality, direct labor is not as variable as we might think, and certainly not as variable as it used to be in assembly line production models.

3. *Cross-training*: The use of average wage rates is based on the assumption that there is an average rate for the person doing the job. In a cellular environment, with cross-training, the rate of the person doing the job can vary widely. Again, traditional cost-based thinking

works against us. Assume we have a cell composed of six workers as follows: one machinist at $35 per hour, one lathe operator at $25 per hour, one welder at $20 per hour, and three assembly workers at $15 per hour. If the assembly workers constantly lag behind and have large piles of WIP to process, do we need to hire another assembly operator? What if the machinist has time to spare and can be trained to do assembly for one-fourth of his time? Why would we pay an employee $35 an hour to do a $15 an hour job? Is not his or her time far too valuable? However, we are paying the machinist regardless; and if we can avoid adding another full-time employee—at any rate—why would we not do so? What if the machinist is not as efficient at assembly as the operators who do this on a regular basis? Is not it still better to use labor that exists in the cell rather than adding labor? In a cellular environment that is focused on lead time, it is better to have cross-trained employees who can move to the bottleneck and shorten lead times than it is to have specialized employees who perform one dedicated function. If you expect to keep everyone in the cell busy 100% of the time, and each team member can only perform one function, and you have variable demand—you *will* create some combination of backlogs, WIP, and finished goods inventory.

Cost of cross-training; paying for skills: Do you need to pay employees more when they acquire additional skills? The answer is yes—although the methodology and rate of increase may vary based on your labor environment and manufacturing process. Think back on the employees who have worked with and for you over your career. Who were the most valuable? What were the characteristics of the ones whom you *couldn't afford to lose*? Did you ever say, *We don't pay him or her enough*? Chances are, when you think about it, the employees in that category were skilled, flexible, and adaptable. They were willing to work where needed and do whatever it took to get the job done. The value of an employee who can fill in for vacations and illness, keep product flowing by moving to bottlenecks, train other employees in skills, and do it all with an understanding of the process and the quality implications at each step—*these are your most valuable employees*. Shouldn't they make more? Even if they do not have to use the skill on a daily basis, the fact they have the skill and are able to fill in as needed is worth recognizing in the form of pay. Their ability to facilitate the team's throughput of quality products, on-time, is more than that of an employee who is not cross-trained.

I have worked in a manufacturing company with a skills matrix, and employees earned increases based on their skills inventory. Employees were eligible for up to an additional $9.00 per hour based on cross-training. I was often asked if I was concerned that we were overpaying employees. My response was always the same. No. If an employee was able to acquire all of the skills (testing, credentialing, and practical application were required to certify in a skill) I was more than happy to write the payroll check, because that employee could contribute at a very high level. What if everyone on the team cross-trained in everything? Wouldn't we be overpaying? The reality is this never happened. Employees have different aptitudes and interests. Acquiring all of the skills requires a significant investment in time and a wide variety of aptitudes ranging from math to an understanding of material properties to team building. There is always some amount of employee turnover. Because of these factors, the probability of an employee certifying in every skill is low, but the value of one who achieves this is immeasurable.

Training does need to be focused, rather than random. The team needs to focus on the skills that are needed within the team to establish throughput, determine where the gaps are, and then determine which team members are best suited to fill the gaps.

A simplistic version of a skills matrix is shown in the following. In reality, skills will be more specific, including use of the computer system modules, quality criteria, team skills, and so on. (The matrix I worked with included a total of 80 skills worth 180 points; each 10 points was equivalent to $.50 per hour for a total range of $9.00 per hour.) Remember that the numbers are people who are proficient in the skill, not full-time equivalents. The example shown is for a team of five persons, where everyone is required to credential in measuring (ideal is five team members), but not everyone needs to know how to use the drill press (ideal is two team members) (Figure 7.1).

Skill	Assembly	Machining	Drilling	Measuring	Root cause analysis	Training	Total
Ideal	4	3	2	5	3	2	19
Actual	2	2	2	5	4	2	17
Gap	2	1	0	0	−1	0	2
Percent of ideal							89%

FIGURE 7.1
Example of a skills matrix.

Within the skill of *Machining,* ideally three team members have this skill. Since only two employees currently qualify for the machining skill, there is a gap of one employee to be trained and certified in machining. All five team members are skilled in measuring; however, various team members each hold other subsets of skills. For any skill, there should be no fewer than two team members who are competent in that skill to allow for backup as well as continuity should a team member leave the team. The *ideal* number is based on the best mix of skills to minimize manufacturing critical path time (MCT).

Members of this team should determine who is best suited to learn machining and assembly, which reflects the gaps identified for the team.

Cross-trained employees are crucial for more than just throughput and bottlenecks. Cross-trained employees develop an understanding of the process—they know how what an operator does in one step can impact another operator at the next step. Because of this, they are valuable participants in continuous improvement projects and often offer ways to do things better. They understand that even if it does not personally save them time, how it may save total time (Manufacturing Critical Path Time), which serves the customer.

Staffing for peak: Cross-training is one way to add spare capacity without adding labor. Continuous improvement projects and eliminating white space are also great ways to create capacity without adding more employees. As volume grows, there will be a point where labor must be added. How can you determine when you have reached that point? In order to meet demand without incurring backlog, late deliveries, and/or inventory, you must staff sufficiently to handle peak demand rather than average demand. This is because if you staff for the average demand, you will create backlogs and late deliveries in times of peak demand. In a complex, make-to-order environment, determining the staffing required for peak demand is not as simple as it sounds. Here are some tips for determining how to staff at peak demand:

- Use your Bill of Material (BOM) labor calculations and keep track of MCT. Use historical tracking of the correlation between total labor hours required to process open orders as specified in the BOM, actual lead time, and labor hours available. You should see the point where lead time is impacted negatively and open order backlog grows. This is peak. If you operate a cross-trained cell, it is not necessary to evaluate by labor type; rather, evaluate total hours. In the analysis in the following, for a cell with five persons and 200 h per week, over a 12-week

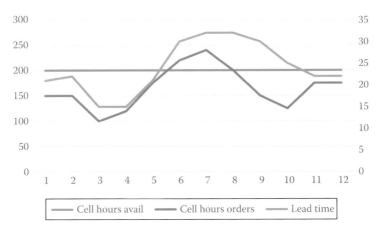

FIGURE 7.2
Peak labor capacity analysis.

period, the cell was overcapacity and lead time suffered beginning in week 6. In this case, in order to maintain lead time, the cell should staff for peak demand at 240 h of 6 full time equivalents (FTEs) (Figure 7.2).

What will team members do in weeks 3–5 when demand is low and only 4 FTEs are required? This is the time for cross-training, continuous improvement projects, team events, and so on.

- Use a rapid modeling tool* to evaluate the best mix of skills to attain *ideal*. A tool of this nature enables you to input actual work orders, routings, and times and perform what-if analysis that will help evaluate the impact of cross-training. This will help establish the ideal mix of skills and number of employees in the cell that will maximize throughput and minimize lead time.

Data collection for labor: In order to have reliable data for capacity planning, and to verify the original estimates used for pricing, it is important that the BOM reflects actual and this includes labor. However, be careful not to add complex data gathering requirements, especially if operators cover multiple machines and operations simultaneously. Having an operator clock in and out as they move machine to machine and process to process is time consuming and will negatively impact throughput. Using the system to allocate labor between processes and machines is prone to error and will not represent actual. Always consider, does the end justify the means? Direct labor, after all, is generally less than 10% as a percent

---

* An example of one such tool is Value Stream Modelling, which is sold by Build to Demand Inc.

of sales and less than 20% as a percent of total cost. Spending inordinate amounts of time and effort to collect this data simply does not make sense. Simple feedback loops, like red-lined times and notes on the work order which are submitted for review and update, make more sense. Random time studies can also be used to supplement estimated labor requirements and times. The workers doing the job know which jobs take significantly more time than allowed, just as they know which jobs consume significantly less time. Open the communication lines and let workers provide the estimates or conduct time studies on a random or targeted basis.

Labor in BOM: Therefore, you should continue to estimate the labor required (in time per piece) and carry this in your BOM. The reason to do so is not for product costing purposes, nor for labor efficiency reports. Use this data, first and foremost, as part of your capacity planning. Historical records of this data will show what peak demand is and give guidance as to staffing levels. It will also provide information for the *feedback loop* that compares quoted to actual and assists with corrective actions when the actual results are significantly different than first estimated.

Labor efficiency is ingrained in U.S. manufacturing and is widely used both by operations managers *and* accountants. As I walk through production facilities, particularly assembly operations, it is rare *not* to see efficiency charts and graphs. Many attempt to justify this by setting the target at something below 100%, say 80%. However, real life says that variability—both in demand and individual job labor requirements—will cause the number to fluctuate and to shoot for any specific target, whether 80% or 100%, is unwise. Focus instead on having the right amount of labor to adjust to variability in demand and maintain lead time targets.

Throughout the remainder of this book, there will be references to direct labor as a component of variable cost. This should not be misinterpreted to imply that if you maintain direct labor costs, labor efficiency calculations are then valid. Direct labor is included only because for purposes of certain analyses, that is, contribution per product, it can provide meaningful information when there is a rational basis for assigning labor to products that does not involve allocations.

> ### Think About It.
>
> Are you afraid to invest money training employees because they might leave? Shouldn't you be more concerned about the consequences if you don't train them and they stay?

8

Simplified Time-Based Accounting

A simplified time-based accounting system (STBA) combines the best of value stream (Lean) accounting and throughput accounting (TA). One central fact these approaches agree on is that product cost with full absorption of overhead (no matter how allocated) distorts true contribution, which can result in faulty profitability analysis, lead to incorrect pricing and make/buy decisions, and often motivates nonproductive behavior.

The recommended approach resolves the criticism of Lean accounting—a total disregard for capturing detailed product costs. Critics point out that the Lean accounting approach provides insufficient information for product pricing, profitability, and make/buy analysis. Everything required for the STBA system resides somewhere in your enterprise resource planning system:

- Bills of material—expected processing times and setup times
- Detail invoice lines—revenue and quantity by product
- Production records—setup time, processing start and processing end, quantity made

No complicated data collection or macro-level to micro-level variance analysis is required. However, the way you think about your bill of material may need to change. The data in your bill of material, particularly involving operators and flow times, may need to change. Flat bills of material that represent the entire process, start to finish, are preferable as they present the entire process. This promotes process thinking and prevents suboptimizing the overall process in favor of local optimization.

The bills of material should represent expected, or average, times—not the best possible. In other words, a real life average. If you have a cross-trained cell and lead times may be shortened by having a less skilled operator do a task, then the bill should represent that time—not the shortest time by the most skilled operator.

The basic premises for STBA:

- The concepts work best in a *cellular environment*, or at a minimum, when considering the entire product flow from start to finish, not isolated processes or departments. A *cell* can be defined as a value stream with resources colocated and committed to the cell, giving control of the entire production process to the cell.
- *Manufacturing critical path time (MCT) is the primary metric.* However, both velocity and MCT are important and the combination of the two is a powerful multiplier for results.
- *Value is added only by making orders.* That is why the calculation is based on actual revenue and products that have shipped. Regardless of balance sheet treatment, inventory is a liability, not an asset. Making product with no immediate sales outlet—in lieu of product that can be sold—is rarely a good decision if you are concerned about cash flow and lead time. Throughput must be based on *shipments* rather than production levels.
- *Costs must include only variable costs*, or those that can be calculated at an item level without allocation. The best example of a truly variable cost is raw material which is generally the most significant variable cost. In assembly operations, an argument may be made that direct labor is a significant component of cost which directly varies with volume and should be included. Few costs beyond these can be considered as variable costs.
- *Production MCT* is the MCT time in the cell. This includes the time work is authorized until the time the product leaves the cell (gray space and white space) and must assume that all activities are completed from *scratch* so that making WIP and parts ahead cannot shorten the lead time. Orders should be time stamped when they are authorized for production as the starting point. Orders should not be authorized for production until all resources are available to complete the order, and orders should not be authorized to start before they are needed. The ending point is when the order is complete and is shipped to the customer.
- *Gray space* is the hours that are spent actively working on the product. These hours include setup time because setup is required before work can begin on the product. Hours are determined based on the longest time to complete the process. For example, in an injection molding process, process time is determined based on setup time plus machine time. Operators may cover many machines, and the length

of the gray space is based on the time on the machine. In an assembly operation, the process time may be determined based on the operator assembly time. For a molded part that goes to assembly, total process time would be setup time plus molding machine time plus assembly time. This reflects *elapsed time* during which the product is actively being worked on or the elapsed time that would be shown on the MCT map. If a product runs unattended or requires less than a dedicated operator, the hours are machine hours. For operations that require an operator rather than a machine, the hours are labor hours.

- *Contribution dollars* equal revenue minus variable costs.

Knowing this information, the contribution per hour of gray space (process hour) can be calculated for any product, group of products, and the cell. You may recognize the calculation from TA with minor adjustments. In this case, hours are process hours—not just hours on the Capacity Constraint Resource. While the Theory of Constraints would argue that the only relevant time is at the bottleneck, or constraint, most operations personnel in a cellular organization with high-mix and custom products recognize that the constraint changes—several times a day!

Referring to Figure 8.1, product A contributes $65 (to cover overhead, selling general and administrative costs, and profit) for every hour we spend processing it. This gives us an idea of the contribution of a product that incorporates the concept of time and also contribution without the distortion of allocations. This analysis is helpful for quoting and pricing decisions, product profitability, and make or buy analysis.

Another type of analysis, or contribution per day of lead time, is appropriate for assessing the trend and magnitude of lead time reductions and velocity. The Contribution per Day of Lead Time assesses the success of shortening "the timeline from the moment the customer gives us an order to the point when we collect the cash" (Taichi Ohno).

A Product	B Revenue	C Variable cost	D (B – C) Contribution per unit	E Process time (h)	F (D/E) Contribution per process hour ($)
A	100	35	65	1	65.00
B	145	45	100	5	20.00
C	175	65	110	2.5	44.00

FIGURE 8.1
Contribution per process hour.

A Order	B Order date	C Ship date	D MCT	E Revenue ($)	F Materials ($)	G Direct labor ($)	H = D − (E + F + G) Contribution ($)	I = H/D Cont./day of MCT ($)
1	8/11/2014	8/15/2014	4	10,000	5,000	1,250	3,750	938
2	8/1/2014	8/15/2014	14	15,000	8,000	1,500	5,500	393
3	7/15/2014	8/15/2014	31	12,500	2,500	1,250	8,750	282
4	7/25/2014	8/15/2014	21	7,500	4,000	1,000	2,500	119
5	8/8/2014	8/15/2014	7	5,000	1,000	500	3,500	500
Total			77	50,000	20,500	5,500	24,000	312

FIGURE 8.2
Contribution per day of lead time (MCT).

The calculations are similar, but rather than dividing by Gray Space, the division is over MCT (lead time) days. The chart shows how orders can be aggregated in a pool, where the total contribution of the pool (revenue – direct costs) is divided by the sum of the lead time days for orders in the pool (Figure 8.2).

Increases in Contribution per Day clearly translate to cash and results. The higher the number, the better. Increases in the contribution numerator will improve the number. Increases in the numerator can be achieved by increasing velocity and reducing costs. Reductions in the MCT denominator will improve the number. Reductions in the denominator can be achieved by elimination of white space.

8.1 MAKE OR BUY DECISIONS

Let us take a look at how these concepts might be used in a make or outsource decision. The following is an actual example (unfortunately) of a decision made to send work outside using product cost (Figure 8.3).

The following part costs were recorded by the cost accounting system:

An outsource vendor indicated that they would produce the part for $65. At first blush, it appears that they can make it $10 cheaper (internal cost of $75 compared to their cost of $65). What is wrong with this analysis? Moving the production to another vendor does not reduce overhead! Depending how *variable* direct labor is, we may have actually saved only the material cost of $32 per unit, for which we are paying $65 per unit. Instead of making $25 per unit, we are now losing $3 per unit (Figure 8.4).

Incorporating contribution per hour into the analysis adds even more information. If each part requires 2 h to manufacture, this product generates $32 per hour (Figure 8.5).

If the work is being outsourced for capacity reasons, now the relevant question is not whether the outsource vendor can do it *cheaper* on a total cost basis, but whether we will replace the work internally with something that has a higher contribution.

> **Common cost misconception**
>
> If you stop producing the part, you no longer incur the fixed costs. This is a faulty assumption that motivates over-production.

Price ($)	100
Material ($)	32
Direct labor ($)	5
Overhead ($)	38
Total cost ($)	75
Profit ($)	25

FIGURE 8.3
Product cost with overhead.

Price ($)	100
Purchase cost ($)	65
Overhead ($)	38
Total cost ($)	103
Profit ($)	−3

FIGURE 8.4
Outsourced cost.

Price ($)	100
Material ($)	32
Direct labor ($)	5
Contribution ($)	63
Hours ($)	2
Contribution/h ($)	32

FIGURE 8.5
Product contribution per hour.

8.2 CELL CONTRIBUTION

What you measure matters. Measurements must be tested to see what behaviors (intended or unintended) are motivated. In a time-based strategy, the desired outcomes are customer responsiveness and throughput. The combination of reduced lead time and increased velocity can produce dramatic results, but how do we measure it?

In a cellular environment, it is important to have measures for the cell. Otherwise, good results of the cell may be masked or offset by results in other areas and the cell will not get the recognition it deserves for reducing lead time and responding to customers.

The customer responsiveness of the cell can only be measured by MCT. All activities to eliminate white space *on the critical path* produce good results. These activities can be viewed as belonging to one of two categories:

1. Activities that eliminate white space by eliminating wait time or queues
2. Activities that eliminate white space with the potential for increasing throughput

Activities that eliminate white space by eliminating queues find a way to move a job through the system with minimal wait time. What is in the white space? Does this mean people are not working? The MCT map shows the average for any one job. Generally, what is in the white space is gray space from other jobs that are being processed while this job waits in queue for the next step or process, or for the rest of the lot (or batch) to finish before it can move to the next step. White space can be reduced by finding ways to move the job through the system in a continuous fashion. Activities in this category include cross-training to eliminate potential bottlenecks, smaller lot sizes, cellular organization structure to eliminate handoffs, and flattened bills of material for continuous flow from start to finish. These activities add great value in the form of reduced inventory, cash flow, and reduced lead times (customer responsiveness). Take the following example. Assume we have a 15-day lead time with 80% white space, that is, 3 days of 15 represent gray space or touch time. The present state MCT map (an average of all orders) looks like this (Figure 8.6).

Assume the average output for a week is 5 orders that average 15 days of lead time as shown. If we are able to eliminate white space, and make the same 5 orders after eliminating white space, the map looks like this (Figure 8.7).

Office processes		Process flow — Fabrication operations	Pack and ship		
2 days	1 day	9 days	1 day	1 day	1 day

15 day lead time; white space 12/15 = 80%

FIGURE 8.6
Present state MCT map.

Process flow →

Office	Fabricate	Pack	Office	Fabricate	Pack	Office	Fabricate	Pack	Office	Fabricate	Pack	Office	Fabricate	Pack
1 day	1 day	1 day	1 day	1 day	1 day	1 day	1 day	1 day	1 day	1 day	1 day	1 day	1 day	1 day
Order 1			Order 2			Order 3			Order 4			Order 5		

+ 12 days order to bill

+ 9 days order to bill

+ 6 days order to bill

+ 3 days order to bill

Cash cycle improved by 30 days!

FIGURE 8.7
Future state MCT map.

Eliminating white space simply by eliminating queues and processing an order completely from start to finish creates velocity—in the form of reducing the order to cash cycle time. Order to cash time is improved as the first order is shipped out 12 days earlier, the next 9 days earlier, and so on—resulting in a 30-day improvement (12 + 9 + 6 + 3). Eliminating white space also reduces both finished goods and WIP inventory. Finished goods are reduced as product is ready to ship much earlier. WIP is reduced as product is converted to finished goods immediately. Most importantly, the customer now has a 3-day lead time—for the same order that used to take 15 days. This scenario has real bottom-line benefits and is achieved primarily by not committing resources to work until the work can be finished without queues and WIP. There are many techniques to achieve this result, beyond the scope of this book, but at the end of the day the lesson is do not start what you cannot finish. As soon as you commit resources (in the form of people, materials, and equipment) to something that cannot be finished, you have created queues and WIP. In this example, we have increased *velocity* (order turns in the form of days from receipt to cash), but the *throughput* of the cell (five orders) remains unchanged.

The second type of white space elimination activities are those that also have the potential for increasing throughput. These activities include finding a whole new way of doing a job, streamlining process flow, reducing change over time, reducing scrap and rework, eliminating travel time by storing supplies at point of use, and good organization of the workplace. Lead time reductions accomplished with these activities have the potential for increasing throughput because time has been removed from the system.

The most important test for a cell metric is that it is based on orders shipped rather than production. Measuring throughput, on its own, can motivate creation of inventory. If throughput is gained by putting products on shelves, it should not be rewarded. If throughput is gained by producing long runs while customer orders are waiting behind the long run, it should not be rewarded. If throughput is gained while responding to customers with quicker turnaround on orders, it *should* be rewarded. If the actions of the cell are improving flow and processes, they will increase throughput which will create capacity that can be turned into revenue. However, if the cell is measured on throughput alone, they will run product regardless of need and regardless of the impact on lead time.

Measuring throughput is problematic in a high-mix environment with demand variation. First, what is the unit of measure? Is the measure units of production? In most high-mix environments, units (i.e., each or piece) can be like adding apples and oranges, since the resources required for any unit can vary widely. Is the measure revenue? This has the same *apples and oranges* problem as units, since the highest revenue items may or may not reflect the actual contribution when the costs (and time) required for to make the unit also vary. Is the measure labor hours absorbed? This is problematic because the calculation assumes the following:

1. Labor standards are accurate.
2. Bottom-line contribution will improve (or worsen) with labor. Since labor is a small percentage of total revenue, the correlation of direct labor and bottom-line contribution is not always readily apparent.
3. Finally, labor absorption is based on units produced—not units sold.

Perhaps the best measure of throughput in a high-mix environment is the contribution of the cell over a stated period of time. When that period of time is MCT, throughput is measured based on both time (MCT) and dollars (contribution).

With reduction in lead time as the strategy, combined with revenue and bottom-line growth, this measure provides the linkage between operations (tactical) and bottom-line results and demonstrates progress to achieving the goals of the organization:

- *MCT* of the cell as the measure of customer responsiveness.
- *Contribution* of the cell based on revenue less totally variable costs. This removes the variability of material content and puts products in the cell on an even footing.
- *Contribution/Day of MCT* as a measure that combines lead time and contribution in the form of how much the cell contributes per day of lead time. The cell can improve the metric by reducing lead time and also by increasing throughput.

The cell generally does not control pricing nor incoming orders. The cell does have a significant impact on bottom-line results by reducing lead time and increasing throughput. These can be measured and tied directly to results using the contribution per day of MCT.

Contribution is measured after deducting variable costs from revenue. This helps eliminate mix problems created by high material content and variability in material costs.

The following definitions will be applied in some scenarios to illustrate the concept of cell contribution per day of MCT:

- Throughput = Contribution of *orders shipped*. Contribution is revenue minus total variable costs (either material alone or material plus direct labor).
- Cell MCT Total = MCT for the time under control of the cell. If the cell is responsible for ordering all materials and scheduling of production, MCT should include raw material procurement time. If the cell does not control raw material procurement and works on orders as released from scheduling, MCT is the period of time from release date to ship date. The total is the sum of MCT for orders shipped for the cell, that is, if 5 orders ship, each with 3 days of lead time, the cell MCT total is 15 days. If 5 orders ship, each with 15 days of lead time, the cell MCT total is 75 days.
- Cell MCT Average = Cell MCT Total divided by the number of orders. For the example given earlier, 15 days/5 orders = 3 days MCT; or 75 days/5 orders = 15 days.
- Velocity Metric or Contribution per Day of MCT: In physics, the formula for velocity is distance divided by time. The result is speed or the distance traveled for a set amount of time. In operational terms, use the formula *Contribution divided by Lead Time*, where contribution is the measure of distance and MCT is the measure of time. The result is the contribution per day of lead time.

Referring to Figure 8.8, the base case is the example used in Chapter 3 where this concept was introduced. The cell ships five orders on August 15 that contribute $24,000 after covering direct costs. The cell averages 15.4 days of lead time, for a total pool of 77 days. The contribution per day of MCT is $24,000/77 = $312 per day of MCT.

In Scenario A, the cell is able to reduce MCT by one day. They produce the same five orders contributing $24,000 after covering direct costs; however, they average 14.4 days of lead time, with a total pool of 72 days. The contribution per day of MCT is $24,000/72 = $333 per day of MCT (Figure 8.9).

Base case

A Order	B Order date	C Ship date	D MCT	E Revenue ($)	F Materials ($)	G Direct labor ($)	H = D − (E + F + G) Contribution ($)	I = H/D Cont/MCT ($)
1	8/11/2014	8/15/2014	4	10,000	5,000	1250	3,750	938
2	8/1/2014	8/15/2014	14	15,000	8,000	1500	5,500	393
3	7/15/2014	8/15/2014	31	12,500	2,500	1250	8,750	282
4	7/25/2014	8/15/2014	21	7,500	4,000	1000	2,500	119
5	8/8/2014	8/15/2014	7	5,000	1,000	500	3,500	500
			77	50,000	20,500	5500	24,000	312
		Average	15.4					1558

FIGURE 8.8

Contribution per day of MCT—base case.

A Order	B Order date	C Ship date	D MCT	E Revenue ($)	F Materials ($)	G Direct labor ($)	H = D − (E + F + G) Contribution ($)	I = H/D Cont/MCT ($)
1	8/11/2014	8/14/2014	3	10,000	5,000	1,250	3,750	1250
2	8/1/2014	8/14/2014	13	15,000	8,000	1,500	5,500	423
3	7/15/2014	8/14/2014	30	12,500	2,500	1,250	8,750	292
4	7/25/2014	8/14/2014	20	7,500	4,000	1,000	2,500	125
5	8/8/2014	8/14/2014	6	5,000	1,000	500	3,500	583
			72	50,000	20,500	5,500	24,000	1667
		Average	14.4					

FIGURE 8.9
Contribution per day of MCT—reduce MCT by 1 day.

In Scenario B, the cell does not reduce lead time, but improves throughput so that the cell is able to ship out six orders with a contribution of $30,250 after covering direct costs in the pool of 92.4 days of MCT. The contribution per day of MCT is $30,250/92.4 = $327 per day of MCT (Figure 8.10).

In Scenario C, the cell reduces lead time by one day for a pool of 86.4 days *and* also improves throughput for a contribution of $30,250. The contribution per day of MCT is $30,250/86.4 = $350 per day of MCT (Figure 8.11).

MCT measures lead time reduction based on elimination of white space. Velocity measures how we can use lead time reduction to create throughput, generate cash, and contribute to the bottom line. This does not imply working faster or being busy all the time. It is a measure of the bottom-line impact of reducing the time from order to cash. The focus is on *orders* that have been *shipped* rather than goods produced that sit in inventory. Although the cell does not directly control orders, the cell can control the production of orders and the timing, scheduling, and flow of production. There is a negative impact on the velocity metric with 100% utilization of resources because this will slow the response time and extend the time to convert orders to cash.

Additionally, eliminating white space creates the very real opportunity for enhanced throughput, because when activities created by the *white space* (counting, checking, changing, planning, expediting, stocking, etc.) are eliminated, there is more time for value-added activities.

Suri [*It's About Time*] also points out that with reduced lead times, the fixed overhead as well as SG&A is likely to be reduced also. With quicker lead times, there will be less expediting of orders, less inventory to track and manage, less inventory obsolescence, less need for planning and scheduling meetings, less renegotiation of due dates with customers, lesser space required for inventory storage, and so on. While it is difficult to draw a direct relationship between these items and lead times, empirical data from actual projects bears out this premise. For further information, refer to "What Kind of 'Numbers' can a Company Expect after Implementing Quick Response Manufacturing? Empirical data from several projects on Lead Time Reduction" by Francisco Turbino and Rajan Suri. This publication can be downloaded from the QRM website at http://qrm.engr.wisc.edu/index.php/research/case-studies.

These savings can be viewed as a bonus on top of the benefits of velocity, potential sales revenue, and customer satisfaction that comes with reduced lead times.

A Order	B Order date	C Ship date	D MCT	E Revenue ($)	F Materials ($)	G Direct labor ($)	H = D − (E + F + G) Contribution ($)	I = H/D Cont/MCT ($)
1	8/11/2014	8/15/2014	4	10,000	5,000	1250	3,750	938
2	8/1/2014	8/15/2014	14	15,000	8,000	1500	5,500	393
3	7/15/2014	8/15/2014	31	12,500	2,500	1250	8,750	282
4	7/25/2014	8/15/2014	21	7,500	4,000	1000	2,500	119
5	8/8/2014	8/15/2014	7	5,000	1,000	500	3,500	500
6	7/31/2014	8/15/2014	15.4	12,000	4,500	1250	6,250	406
			92.4	62,000	25,000	6750	30,250	327
		Average	15.4					1964

FIGURE 8.10

Contribution per day of MCT—improve throughput.

A Order	B Order date	C Ship date	D MCT	E Revenue ($)	F Materials ($)	G Direct labor ($)	H = D − (E + F + G) Contribution ($)	I = H/D Cont/MCT ($)
1	8/11/2014	8/14/2014	3	10,000	5,000	1250	3,750	1250
2	8/1/2014	8/14/2014	13	15,000	8,000	1500	5,500	423
3	7/15/2014	8/14/2014	30	12,500	2,500	1250	8,750	292
4	7/25/2014	8/14/2014	20	7,500	4,000	1000	2,500	125
5	8/8/2014	8/14/2014	6	5,000	1,000	500	3,500	583
6	7/31/2014	8/14/2014	14.4	12,000	4,500	1250	6,250	434
			86.4	62,000	25,000	6750	30,250	350
		Average	14.4					2101

FIGURE 8.11

Contribution per day of MCT—reduce MCT by 1 day *and* improve throughput.

8.3 SAMPLE CONTRIBUTION FINANCIAL STATEMENT PRESENTATION

For financial reporting purposes, the results of the cell should be presented as a value stream, with the contribution to the bottom line after covering variable costs. Variable cost components vary depending on the business model and may include material only, or in other cases, may include both material and direct labor. In Figure 8.12, note that no attempt is made to allocate costs that are not attributable to the cell. These values are reported in the *Total* column and should not be *allocated* to cells. Any allocation is arbitrary and leads to erroneous assumptions about the income or loss of the cell. The actual format for detailed statements would break out in detail the line items that comprise *variable cost* (i.e., material and direct labor), *fixed overhead* (i.e., rent, depreciation), and *SG&A* (i.e., salaries, selling expenses).

Production hours on Line D must be the hours consumed to produce the revenue recorded on Line A. These are the hours consumed in Cost of Goods Sold. Mixing current period production hours with sales that may or may not have been made in the same period will skew the data in a high-mix environment. Standard hours can be used in lieu of actual hours, but your system must be able to identify the production hours that correlate to product sales.

Note the distinction between *Contribution per Production Hour* and *Contribution per Day of MCT*. Contribution per Production Hour shows what is being contributed per hour of run time. This number shows the

		Cell A	Cell B	Cell C	Total
A	Revenue	$100,000	$250,000	$175,000	$525,000
B	Variable cost	$35,000	$100,000	$135,000	$270,000
$C = A - B$	Contribution	$65,000	$150,000	$40,000	$255,000
D	Production hours	1,800	2,000	1,500	5,300
$E = C/D$	Contribution/ production hour	$36.11	$75.00	$26.67	$48.11
F	Cumulative MCT days	100	250	175	525
$G = C/F$	Contribution/day of MCT	$650	$600	$229	$486
H	Fixed overhead				$75,000
I	SG&A				$105,000
$J = C - H - I$	Profit				$75,000

FIGURE 8.12
Cell contribution per day of MCT.

potential contribution of additional run hours in the cell, assuming there is capacity available. The Contribution per Day of MCT shows how the cell is doing at reducing lead time and improving throughput based on orders presented to the cell.

8.4 INCREMENTAL CONTRIBUTION

One word of caution is that Cell C should not be assumed to be under-performing because it has the lowest contribution. It may simply mean that the products of that cell are commodity items and are more competitively priced. Rather, trends that use a comparison to a baseline can help to determine if the results are improving. The supplemental schedule shown in Figure 8.13 calculates an incremental contribution based on change from the baseline. This shows how the cells are doing at eliminating white space

		Cell A	Cell B	Cell C	Total
A	Revenue	$100,000	$250,000	$175,000	$525,000
B	Variable cost	$35,000	$100,000	$135,000	$270,000
C = A − B	Contribution	$65,000	$150,000	$40,000	$255,000
D	Production hours	1,800	2,000	1,500	5,300
E = C/D	Contribution/production hour	$36.11	$75.00	$26.67	$48.11
F	Cumulative MCT days	100	250	175	525
G = C/F	Contribution/day of MCT	$650	$600	$229	$486
H = G/24	Contribution/hour of MCT	$27.08	$25.00	$9.52	$20.24
I = F*24	Total MCT in hours	2,400	6,000	4,200	12,600
J	Baseline cumulative MCT in hours	3,000	6,000	5,200	14,200
K	Baseline contribution	$65,000	$135,000	$30,000	$230,000
L = K/J	Baseline contribution/MCT hour	$21.67	$22.50	$5.77	$16.20
M = H − L	Incremental contribution/MCT hour	$5.42	$2.50	$3.75	$4.04
N = M*I	Incremental contribution	$13,000	$15,000	$15,769	$50,915
O = L*I	Check: if no change in rate	$52,000	$135,000	$24,231	$204,085
		$65,000	$150,000	$40,000	$255,000

FIGURE 8.13
Incremental contribution.

and increasing throughput *and* what the value of that means to bottom-line contribution. The examples presented show three different scenarios.

Cell A maintains the same contribution, but does this in fewer cumulative MCT hours. In other words, the cell generates the same contribution in less time. This represents the value added by lead time reduction.

Cell B generates a higher contribution in the same cumulative MCT hours. This represents the value added by increased throughput.

Cell C generates the highest *incremental* contribution from baseline by doing both, reducing lead time *and* increasing throughput. Even though they have the lowest contribution, incrementally they show the greatest improvement.

The columns from Figure 8.13 are defined as follows:

- Revenue (A) = Sales of products shipped from Cell C production.
- Variable Cost (B) = Costs of Cell C that vary directly with production, for example, material. Often direct labor is included as well.
- Contribution (C) = Revenue (A) minus Variable Cost (B).
- Production Hours (D) = Hours of production required to generate revenue on line (A).
- Contribution per Production Hour (E) = Contribution (C) divided by Production Hours (D).
- Cumulative MCT Days (F) = Sum of lead time days for each order shipped and reported in Revenue on line A. For example, 10 orders averaging 10 days of MCT = Cumulative MCT days of 100.
- Contribution per Day of MCT (G) = Contribution (C) Divided by Cumulative MCT Days (F).
- Contribution per Hour of MCT (H) = Contribution per Day of MCT (G) Divided by 24.
- Total MCT in Hours (I) = Cumulative MCT Days (F) × 24.
- Baseline Cumulative MCT in Hours (J) = Cumulative MCT in hours established at the beginning of the reporting period for comparison purposes. For example, the average of the last quarter may be used as the baseline for the following quarter. Alternatively, the average of the prior year may be used as the baseline for the following year.
- Baseline Contribution (K) = Contribution (revenue minus variable costs) for the period that corresponds to the baseline period selected. If the baseline period is the prior year, the baseline contribution should be the average contribution per reporting period for the prior year.

- Baseline Contribution per Hour of MCT (L) = Baseline Contribution (K) divided by Baseline Cumulative MCT in Hours (J).
- Incremental Contribution per Hour of MCT (M) = Contribution per Hour of MCT (H) minus Baseline Contribution per Hour of MCT (L). This represents the increase (or decrease) of the contribution per hour of MCT in the cell. In this example, Cell A is now contributing $27.08 per hour of MCT, compared to $21.67 at baseline. This represents an increase of $5.42 for every hour of MCT.
- Incremental Contribution in Dollars (N) = Incremental Contribution per Hour of MCT (M) times the cumulative MCT in Hours (I). For the 2400 h of cumulative MCT in the cell, the contribution of Cell A is incrementally increased by 2400 times $5.42 or $13,000.
- Check Figure (O) = Determine what the contribution would have been at the baseline MCT Contribution per hour times the cumulative MCT hours. This is what the cell would have contributed at the baseline rate applied to the current cumulative MCT hours. The incremental contribution (N) plus the check figure (O) should equate to the cell contribution.

By using the cumulative MCT days, the calculation is adjusted for volume presented to the cell. *The cell is not penalized for lower volume unless they stretch out the lead time on that volume.*

9

Pricing Strategies under High Mix/Low Volume

Time and Pricing—If you are pricing based on margins or cost plus markup, your pricing does not factor in TIME!

9.1 WHY GROSS PROFIT IS A POOR PREDICTOR OF PROFIT CONTRIBUTION?

Gross profit is what is left after paying for Cost of Goods Sold (COGS). COGS is the accumulated total of all manufacturing costs used to create a product that has been sold. These costs fall into the subcategories of direct labor, materials, and manufacturing overhead. As already discussed, manufacturing overhead is composed of indirect costs. Indirect costs are those that are not directly associated with a manufacturing activity or part. Indirect costs are aggregated into an overhead cost pool and allocated to products. Examples of manufacturing indirect costs are supervision and maintenance wages, equipment repair and maintenance, factory rent, depreciation on factory equipment, and utilities.

Take the example of five parts, each generating $300,000 in revenue, shown in Figure 9.1.

($000s)	A	B	C	D	E	Total
Sales	300	300	300	300	300	1500
Material and labor	150	160	156	156	192	814
Overhead	75	110	42	110	42	379
Gross profit	75	30	102	34	66	307
GP%	25	10	34	11	22	20.5

FIGURE 9.1
Product mix and product cost.

($000s)	A	C	E	Total
Sales	500	500	500	1500
Material and labor	250	260	320	830
Overhead				379
Gross profit				291
GP%				19.4

FIGURE 9.2
Results of eliminating low margin items.

Based on this analysis, we decide that we need to eliminate B and D because of their low contribution (10% and 11%, respectively, compared to 21% overall). Even if we manage to generate the same revenue from the remaining parts, the gross profit actually drops by 1.1% and $16,000 (Figure 9.2).

Why? Because the $379,000 in overhead is a fixed expense, which does not change with the product mix. However, since the products we eliminated were *allocated* to absorb more overhead, we actually lose margin.

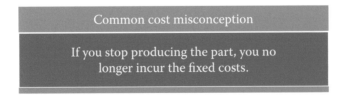

Common cost misconception

If you stop producing the part, you no longer incur the fixed costs.

Had we looked at this on a contribution margin basis, after materials and direct labor but *before* overhead, our product analysis would look different, with the lowest contribution from product E (Figure 9.3).

($000s)	A	B	C	D	E	Total
Sales	300	300	300	300	300	1500
Material and labor	150	160	156	156	192	828
Contribution margin	150	140	144	144	108	672
CM%	50	47	48	48	36	45

FIGURE 9.3
Contribution margin view.

The lesson is that fixed and sunk costs (machines that have already been purchased, rent that will be incurred in any case, insurance costs that are based on existing facilities and equipment, etc.) should not be considered when evaluating product profitability.

Many organizations, in an attempt to motivate their sales force to sell on profitability, rather than volume alone, have structured their commission programs based on gross margin. Again, standard cost and overhead absorption may be working counter to the objective of motivating bottom-line results. We may be rewarding selling the wrong things, because we have not considered velocity and the impact of time!

9.2 WHY MARGINS ARE POOR PREDICTORS OF RESULTS?

The danger of using percentages for product profitability analysis in a high-mix, nonrepetitive, and nonhomogenous environment can be further illustrated by another example. Assume we have a customer that decides to modify their fabricated steel product by adding an expensive electrical component. Assume that we are able to adjust the price for this product to cover the cost of the component. In Figure 9.4, the additional component cost of $250 has been added to the previous selling price of $1000 and the unit is now priced at $1250 to cover the cost of the new component. Shouldn't the margin be the same?.

Looking at the results, based on the drop from 30% to 24% for steel as a percent of sales, you might ask "Did we just save 6% on steel?" Or, based on the margin drop from 70% to 56%, you might ask "Did we just lose 14% in margin?".

	Before		After	
	Dollars	**% of Sales**	**Dollars**	**% of Sales**
Sales	$1000		$1250	
Steel	300	30%	300	24%
Electronics	—		250	
Margin	$700	70%	$700	56%

FIGURE 9.4
Percentages and mix.

Of course, the answer to the question of whether the drop in steel percentage of 6% means we saved money, or whether the margin decrease of 14% means we lost money is neither one. We made $700 before we added the new component and we still made $700 after. The percentages, however, tell a different story. Whether discussing overhead allocations or cost of sales, the same principle applies. The only way the information is valid is with repetitive manufacturing (high volume) with a small number of end items or a very consistent mix. Custom products with varying mix, material content, and volumes cannot be properly priced or evaluated using traditional cost accounting techniques and gross profit margins.

9.3 CONTRIBUTION PRICING?

Pricing is often dictated by the market. Even so, custom manufacturers have to quote pricing for new products on a regular basis. This generally starts with figuring out the cost based on estimated material requirements, projected cycle times, and projected labor requirements. Then a factor or factors are applied to cost to come up with a price. Often the factors may vary based on run times that amortize setup costs and the customer receives bracketed price quotes where they pay less for ordering in higher volumes.

I have observed the use of a complex spreadsheet to calculate overhead rates by machine (machine rates). Each overhead expense line item (i.e., salaries, rent, depreciation, etc.) is distributed across machine(s) using various factors. For example, you might choose to allocate an expense line item based on 50% depreciation and 50% on run hours. The dirty secret is that even after applying what logically made sense, if the resulting rates

A	B	C	D (B – C)	E	F (D/E)
Product	Revenue ($)	Variable cost ($)	Contribution per unit ($)	Process time (h)	Contribution per hour ($)
A	100	35	65	1	65
B	145	45	100	5	20
C	175	65	110	2.5	44

FIGURE 9.5
Contribution per hour.

did not come out to what was expected, the percentages and factors would be manipulated until the expected answer was produced. And these rates were used to develop quotes (prices) for customers!

The use of margins and markups do not properly incorporate the concept of time, as noted earlier. How might we price products and incorporate the concept of time?

Take another look at the calculation of contribution per hour from the prior chapter (Figure 9.5).

What if we calculated pricing based on a targeted contribution per hour? For example, if our operating plan calls for the following:

- $10 million of revenue
- $5 million of variable expenses
- Planned process time of 100,000 h

Then we must expect to average $50 contribution for each hour we run, calculated as (revenue – variable expenses)/process hours:

- ($10,000,000 – $5,000,0000)/100,000 = $50

If we are able to generate an average contribution of $50 per hour of production, and meet our expense budget, we should meet plan.

Therefore, if quoting a part that has $50.00 in variable expenses, that takes 5 h to run, it should be priced using the formula that determines at what price we cover our variable expenses and still generate $50 per hour, as depicted in the following formula:

$$\frac{(X - \$50.00)}{5} = \$50$$

Solving the equation for X,

$$X - \$50 = \$250$$

$$X = \$250 + \$50 = \$300$$

In order to yield \$50 contribution per hour of process time, the part should be priced at \$300.

This formula builds the price based on the known *truly variable cost*, and then adds a factor to cover overhead, SG&A, and profit—without attempting to come up with an individual product-based rate or factor.

Pricing, in any form, must take into consideration how competitors will price the same quote. If, for example, common pricing formulas in the industry incorporate a wide range of machine rates based on the capital-intensive nature of the business, the model can be updated to do the same. In this case, use the calculation above to determine the average contribution rate, and then determine the targets for each group of machines. For example, assume we have work centers with equipment investments and hours as shown in Figure 9.6.

If we expect to make 55% contribution after covering variable costs, and the expected hours for each center are 25,000, then the target rates are calculated as:

$$\text{Expected contribution}(C) = \text{capital}(A) \times \text{target contribution rate}(B)$$

$$\text{Target rate}(E) = \text{expected contribution}(C)/\text{expected hours}(D)$$

In reality, the number of hours and expected contribution rate will vary based on the average contribution of products running in the cell and

		Center 1	Center 2	Center 3	Center 4	Center 5	Total
A	Capital(\$)	1,000,000	2,000,000	3,000,000	4,000,000	5,000,000	15,000,000
B	Target cont. rate (%)	55	55	55	55	55	55
C = A*B	Target cont. (\$)	550,000	1,100,000	1,650,000	2,200,000	2,750,000	8,250,000
D	Hours	25,000	25,000	25,000	25,000	25,000	125,000
E = C/D	Target Rate/Hr (\$)	22.00	44.00	66.00	88.00	110.00	66.00

FIGURE 9.6
Target rates with capital investment options.

	Center 1	Center 2	Center 3	Center 4	Center 5	%
Run size 1	$26.40	$52.80	$79.20	$105.60	$132.00	120
Run size 2	$24.20	$48.40	$72.60	$96.80	$121.00	110
Run size 3	**$22.00**	**$44.00**	**$66.00**	**$88.00**	**$110.00**	**100**
Run size 4	$19.80	$39.60	$59.40	$79.20	$99.00	90
Run size 5	$17.60	$35.20	$52.80	$70.40	$88.00	80

FIGURE 9.7
Contribution targets with run sizes and machine centers.

expected demand. The end result is that target rates reflect the relative capital (and return on capital) that will yield the desired $8,250,000 of contribution that will be required to cover planned fixed costs, selling and general administrative expenses, and desired profit.

The grid can be further expanded to incorporate run sizes, if you believe you can get a premium for short runs. This grid would look something like Figure 9.7, with a separate target for each center and run size combination. The average target for each center is shown in the middle of the grid (Run Size 3), with a premium factor applied to shorter runs (Run Sizes 1 and 2) and a discount factor applied to longer runs (Run Sizes 4 and 5).

9.4 SETUP COST, BATCH SIZES, AND VOLUME DISCOUNTS

Keep in mind that the entire mind-set behind volume pricing is that lower costs are possible by amortizing high setup costs over longer runs. Rather than come up with complex pricing grids for various run sizes, an effective setup reduction program will enable one price for all run sizes. Just think about the power in the market place if your competitors are offering volume pricing, and you are able to offer one competitive price for small lots!

For example, assume you make a part that requires 2 h of setup. The part runs at a speed of 100 parts per hour. The material and direct labor content of the part is $1.00. Setup time is valued at $50 per hour. Traditional volume-based thinking says that we can save $.05 on each part by running twice as much, as shown in Figure 9.8. The $.05 cost reduction is achieved by spreading the $100 setup cost over twice as many units, that is, 2000 instead of 1000. Therefore, we should incentivize our customer to buy in larger lots, right?

Pieces	1000	2000
Piece cost	$1.00	$1.00
Setup time	2	2
Run time	10	20
Setup cost	$100	$100
Part cost	$1000	$2000
Setup + run cost	$1100	$2100
Piece cost	$1.10	$1.05

FIGURE 9.8
Amortizing setup costs.

We know that large lots create waiting and queues. What if, instead of trying to amortize setup, we try to reduce it so we can offer competitive pricing on lower lot sizes? Using the example above, we can *save* the same $.05 by cutting setup in half. If we cut setup time in half from 2 to 1 h, we achieve the same result. We can now offer our customer a competitive price for 1000 units instead of the larger lot of 2000. In doing so, we improve lead time and our competitive position. We can offer our customer the advantage of having to carry lower inventories by ordering in smaller lots. It really is not about saving the nickel. The real bottom-line impact is that by cutting our setup time in half, we can now do twice as many for the same cost! This allows us to produce in smaller lots, carry less inventory, offer competitive prices, and respond to our customers more quickly.

Examples of setup reduction from hours to minutes are well documented. Beginning with Toyota and Single Minute Exchange of Dies there are proven techniques, examples, and specific process changes that can achieve reductions of this magnitude. Mold and die exchange are not that different industry to industry, although handling issues and the cost of solutions do increase as the mold size (and weight) increases. It has been done, and it can be done. Get your setup personnel involved in the effort and make sure they know that by cutting setup times their jobs will not be eliminated.

The combination of reduced setup times and reduced batch sizes can reduce inventory, reduce warehouse space requirements, and improve cash flow—for both the manufacturer and their customers. What would happen if you could offer your customers smaller batches at a price that is competitive with large batch prices of your competitors?

Focusing on increasing lots to amortize setup is putting the focus in the wrong place. If we are trying to motivate actions that reduce lead time and serve the customer, isn't it more productive to focus on reducing change over time?

Tip
Rather than spending time figuring out how to account for long set ups in your product cost, spend time figuring out how to reduce set ups.

10

Is Inventory a Liability or an Asset?

 Definition of "Asset"

Any item of economic value owned by an individual or corporation, especially that which could be converted to cash.

In accounting terms, inventory is considered an asset, because it represents something that can be sold and converted to cash. Orders that have been shipped and invoiced, but are as yet unpaid, are also considered assets (Accounts Receivable). Accounts receivable and inventory are generally the largest component of Current Assets. The category of *Current Assets* is used in most (if not all) calculations of liquidity that assess the ability of a company to cover its current obligations by converting both inventory and receivables into cash to pay bills. An asset is generally considered to be a Current Asset if it can be converted into cash within 1 year.

Unless a manufacturer has unlimited resources and piles of cash, finished goods inventory represents a decision to convert raw materials and labor into a product that cannot be sold immediately over another product that could be. It seems strange (and illogical) that accepted ratio analysis assumes that a company with lots of inventory is in a better position to meet its obligations than one that does not carry inventory.

It may be helpful to think about cash and inventory in the context of the length of the order to cash cycle, which is very similar to the manufacturing critical path time (MCT) calculation except the end of the time interval is when you receive payment rather than when the order is delivered. If you turn your finished goods inventory 10 times a year, you average 36 days of inventory. However, this is just finished goods inventory. If we calculate inventory turns *from scratch* (as defined by MCT) and include the raw materials inventory, the cycle gets longer. If you carry another 60 days of raw materials, you now have 60 days of raw material plus 36 days of finished goods = 96 days of cash tied up. If your customer pays in an average of 45 days, the total cash lead time is 60 + 36 + 45 = 141 days. If we maintain large WIP inventories, we need to add those in as well. This is the *true* order to cash cycle, rather than the traditional view from receipt of order to cash payment from the customer. Long lead times definitely impact both inventory and cash!

Inventory that can be converted into cash in the short term is an asset. The key words in that phrase are *short term*. One year is certainly not *short term* in today's business environment. How many creditors would agree to wait 365 days to get paid while a business sells off its inventory? This probably actually occurs only in reorganization and bankruptcy proceedings!

How might theories of large batch sizes, long runs to minimize setups, and buying in bulk for volume discounts change if inventory was treated as a current asset only in the very short term? What if we had to write down or write off finished goods inventory older than 1 month? This, of course, would not comply with generally accepted accounting principle any more than variable costing (valuing inventory with variable costs only) or throughput costing (valuing inventory with material content only). However, it may be useful to keep such a reserve account (as a contra-account) as a visible reminder of decisions made to invest material, labor, and *time* into something that has not been converted to cash in the real short term, rather than the accounting short term.

What if we adjusted the reserve for obsolescence each month end with product more than 30 days of age?

An example of such an entry would be Figure 10.1.

Account	Classification	Debit	Credit
Inventory over 30 days	Long term asset	×	
Reserve for inventory over 30 days	Current asset		×

FIGURE 10.1
Sample inventory reclassification for inventory aged beyond average cash cycle.

This entry would move inventory over 30 days of age from the Current Asset category to the Long-Term Asset category. While the motivation to absorb costs and build inventory is unchanged, the tie-up of cash and the ability to cover current obligations is reflected more accurately in ratio analysis.

11

More on Simplified Time-Based Accounting

11.1 STOP ABSORBING OVERHEAD AND ELIMINATE STANDARD COST VARIANCE REPORTING

Getting *rid of* standard cost is not the solution in and of itself. Even actual cost systems still allocate overhead to parts to come up with product cost. Why? Because there is no such thing as actual overhead per part! Therefore, in order to produce fully absorbed product costs, whether on a standard or actual basis, the overhead must be allocated. What are the two most important objectives for time-based accounting?

1. Eliminate the allocation of overhead. Whether standard or actual, overhead by part is a fictitious number.
2. Get rid of detailed variance reporting in the financial statements that mask the true cost of material, labor, and overheads while confusing the reader.

These objectives can be attained by various methods, depending on your enterprise resource planning (ERP) system and the costing options within the system. Some options for doing so are described in this chapter.

With or without standard cost, a good manufacturing system requires a solid and accurate bill of material (BOM). Be sure you utilize your BOM capability correctly. The BOM should present *actual* and *not* standard or perfect performance. Bills of material are typically initiated in engineering and are the foundation of the quoted price to customer. At this point in time, they represent a prediction of what the actual resource consumption—and cost—will be for the project or part.

There must be a method to compare the predicted consumption of resources against actual. Why? First, to evaluate pricing and profitability of the part. If resource consumption is significantly more than predicted, there may be an opportunity to make a price adjustment.

In any case, the knowledge of the additional resource consumption is important and may factor into future calculations and adjustments. Second, the adjustment of the BOM to actual resource consumption is necessary for the ERP system (or any capacity planning system) to produce any sort of rough-cut capacity analysis with any degree of reliability. If your ERP system is built on *standard* performance rather than *actual* performance, how can you expect valid capacity planning data?

Often you can use your *standard* cost system as an *actual* cost system. Make sure your bills of material reflect actual material requirements, run rates, and labor requirements.

11.2 FEEDBACK LOOPS

Keeping bills of material accurate requires an effective feedback loop to adjust resource data based on actual experience. Rather than using variance analysis, which is looking in a rear view mirror and requires sifting through thousands of transactions, why not rely on the cell to provide feedback? Expected resource requirements, such as operators, setup time, cycle times, and scrap rates, can be displayed on the job or work order. If the actual experience is different, why not have the cell *red-line* or annotate the work order and return this to engineering (or whoever maintains bills of material)? If the cell is not being evaluated on variances, or their performance against *standard*, they have no motivation to hide this information.

The feedback of the cell should be accepted as the actual consumption of resources. It is difficult to measure performance against an arbitrary standard. Allow the cell to report real life, as it happens, not as recorded in thousands of transactions that require analysis and reporting back to the cell—often weeks later—regarding what accounting thinks happened based on data that does not consider system dynamics and the interaction between resources (people, machines, and materials).

Labor data should only be collected using data collection methods IF the results are reliable *and* if the data collection method is simple and takes little to no operator time. For example, if an operator works on multiple machines and work orders at one time, data collection is not reliable because either the operator spends all day clocking in and out of jobs *or* you are allocating time (and by now I hope the problems with allocation in a high-mix environment have been well established).

I recently worked with a company where cell operators were spending 400 h a month clocking in and out of work orders—for every part and every process. At a rate of $25 per hour, this amounts to $120,000 per year just to collect labor data. And yet, direct labor was less than 10% of revenue. The following options were recommended to eliminate this cost and still maintain accurate labor data in bills of material:

1. Allow the ERP system to consume, or absorb, labor data at standard for purposes of product cost. For purposes of reporting labor cost in the cell, and in total, use actual payroll data.
2. Perform selected (random and/or targeted) time studies to validate bills of material.
3. Print standard times on the work order and ask the cell to report significant variances by red-lining the work order.
4. Make it easy for the cell to perform select timings. A digital timer with a start and stop button is low cost and requires very little time to use. The operator can easily compare actual results to the work order in this manner.

11.3 REPLACE VARIANCE ANALYSIS WITH IMPROVEMENT ACTIVITIES

Turn off detailed variance reporting and daily accumulation of transactions into variance accounts. Allocate the amount of time you would have spent each month in analyzing variances to continuous improvement projects. Even accounting activities have white space and there are lots of opportunities in the office. Labor variances by item (in detail) can be turned off by consuming at standard as described earlier. Overhead variances can be eliminated by setting the overhead rate to zero and making one overhead entry rather than attempting to allocate to products.

To do this, turn off the options in your ERP system that record detail standard cost transactions of costs absorbed and shipped (along with variances from standard) with each and every production and shipping record.

One concern is the loss of perpetual inventories. In fact, all that is lost is the perpetual *dollar* inventory which is maintained by adding and subtracting the value of each transaction. Perpetual *quantities* are still maintained and inventory values at any point in time may still be calculated by extending quantities by cost. Inventory values can be adjusted with simple entries for financial reporting at month and/or year end.

11.4 SIMPLIFY BILLS OF MATERIAL

Multilevel bills of material are problematic. How are costs transferred from one level to another? Do material costs accumulate in material costs and do labor costs accumulate in labor costs? Or, do all the costs from the previous process (labor, material, and overhead) go into the next process as material cost?

Each level of a BOM is an opportunity for work in process (WIP). The first level bill has an output, which becomes an input to another process or level. A work order will generate for the quantity needed at the next step in the process. The WIP created will sit until the work order to process the product at the next step comes up in the queue. When the processes have independent owners, metrics, personnel, and flow rates—there is even more opportunity for WIP from the one level to sit at the next level.

Flattening bills of material is more than an exercise in ERP system maintenance. Reducing the number of levels can reduce costs and shorten lead times by eliminating activities associated with each level as related to opening work orders, moving materials in and out of stock, and reporting production at each process level. Flattening the BOM implies that all of the processes to produce the end item are contained within one cell, with one owner, and evaluated with one set of metrics.

For example, assume we make a part that goes through four work centers, forming, drilling, painting, and assembly. The following example of a formed part holds true for any part that moves from machine to machine, or department to department, and where different processes or operations are performed. First parts are formed (molded, extruded), shown as Part A and Part B. Part A requires drilling of holes. The part with the drilled hole is now Part C. Part B requires painting. The painted part is now Part D. The drilled part C and the painted part D are then assembled into finished item E (Figure 11.1).

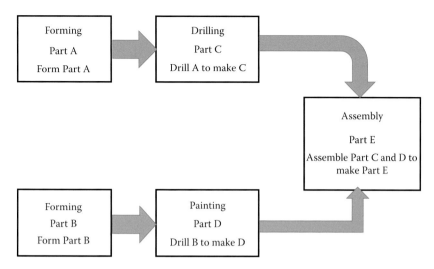

FIGURE 11.1
Three level bill of materials.

To complete the simple assembly shown for this three level BOM, five part numbers are required. Five work orders will be created to complete each part in each work center. As each part moves to the next process or work center, the part will go into WIP along with other work orders waiting for painting, drilling, or assembly.

What if we eliminate just one level of the BOM by co-locating the forming process with the painting and drilling process? Instead of five, we now have three part numbers and three work orders. If we have WIP at all, it will be at Assembly (one spot) rather than three piles of WIP at three work centers (Figure 11.2).

Flat bills of material imply a cellular structure where the production process is encompassed from the start to the finish in one area, under the direction and control of one team. This also implies dedicated equipment, since the cell cannot control the process if they must wait behind other teams (cells) to complete the production process.

Achieving a flat BOM improves cellular reporting and analysis. Capacity planning (both labor and equipment) can be done cell by cell based on a specific group of products and a specific group of materials. It greatly reduces, or even eliminates, WIP—since the cell is responsible for the entire production from start to finish and can allocate resources accordingly. It also improves the feedback loop. When multiple departments, and machines, and BOM levels are involved, feedback can be problematic. "Why should I bother? Assembly never turns in their changes..."

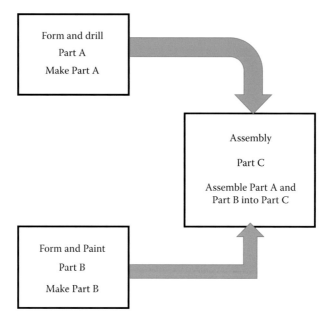

FIGURE 11.2
Simplified two-level bill of materials.

Any accountant who has tried to analyze and verify a rolled up item cost that involves more than three levels knows that simplified bills of material make cost analysis easier. Multilevel bills of material, by virtue of complexity, mask cost sources and complicate the review and analysis of cost data.

11.5 SIMPLIFY MATERIAL

Eliminate purchase price variances and record material costs at the last price paid. This is readily available in your ERP system. As long as your material stocks turn regularly, this will approximate actual cost in inventory.

If the only criterion for your vendors is price, then you are probably buying too much. Looking at price variances—without considering time and quality—masks the true cost of purchasing. Purchasing departments that are evaluated on price variances will buy in quantity. If you add in inventory turns as a measure, now they have the dilemma of whether price or turns is more important.

The Economic Order Quantity (EOQ) formula was developed to mathematically analyze the trade-off between interest (holding cost) and volume discounts in purchasing lot size decisions. When applied to buying decisions, what the EOQ does not consider is the reality that funds are limited; and buying more of one material (even though it is a really good deal) means that you must buy less of another (which may be needed for an order that can ship right away). The EOQ formula also does not consider the potential of obsolescence associated with buying in quantity. Space and warehousing limitations are also not factored into the formula.

If you can get a material from an overseas supplier at half the cost, but it takes 12 weeks to arrive, and you have to order in large quantities because of shipping costs and the time to replenish each order (I will take a full container)—what have you really saved? Yet, the purchase price variance analysis will say this is the right thing to do and reward the buyer.

What is a buyer to do?

- Order what you need.
- Order from reputable suppliers that give you quick delivery and a competitive price.
- If you use report cards, evaluate your supplies on both lead time and quality.

To record material in inventory for any period,

Step 1: Update material costs with last price paid

Allow the cost of materials to flow through to cost of sales based on actual purchases.

Step 2: Calculate material cost by product

Update product cost by recalculating your standard cost. If you have updated your material cost based on most recent price paid, the cost system will now contain material cost by product (using last price paid times standard quantities required). There is no over/under absorption, because costs are at actual. Product in stock, whether WIP or finished goods, will carry a material component based on current purchase costs and quantities required as specified in the BOM.

Step 3: Book inventory journal entry

Run an inventory value report (quantity on hand times cost) which summarizes the value in your closing inventory by cost element, or the sum of your

Account	Debit	Credit
Inventory	$5,000.00	
Material in inventory (COGS)		$5,000.00
Record inventory change for material content		

FIGURE 11.3
Journal entry to record material in inventory.

inventory quantities times cost for material components. Material may be segregated between major material categories or type of material purchase. Compare this month's material in inventory to last month's material in inventory and book an entry for the change (or use a reversing entry and book the entire value as shown on the report). Refer to Figure 11.3 for an example of an entry to record a material content increase in inventory of $5,000.

11.6 SIMPLIFY LABOR

For labor, use actual direct labor dollars as recorded by your payroll system (by cell or in total) to determine the actual labor rate. Then use the operator data and cycle times from your BOM to calculate product cost for labor. If you have implemented feedback loops (without variances), the BOM should be a fairly accurate picture of labor required for any part. If you have defined labor as a *truly variable cost* for your process, then use the system to calculate the direct labor cost per item using the BOM quantities at actual rates.

Use the data from your BOM to estimate the labor in inventory and book one entry at month end for the labor in inventory. (There is a very good chance that this inventory will be more accurate than the entries generated by your standard cost system.)

Step 1: Record actual labor from your payroll system

As with material, allow the actual cost of labor to flow through to cost of sales based on actual payroll.

Step 2: Calculate the labor rate per hour of production

Assuming your inventory turns at least once per month, use direct labor dollars for the month. (For longer periods of time, use payroll data that corresponds to the days in inventory; there is no need to be precise in terms of number of days.)

$$\text{Standard operator hours} = \text{sum of (cycle time} * \text{number of}$$
$$\text{operators required) for production}$$
$$\text{in the period}$$
$$\text{Average labor rate per run hour} = \text{direct labor dollars from}$$
$$\text{payroll/standard operator hours.}$$

Do not expect the number to match your average pay rate. The calculation will vary depending on whether an operator covers several machines, the amount of white space, holidays, and so on. The number is not a metric, the calculation is used to value inventory. The result is a number that will fully absorb all of your direct labor.

Step 3: Update the direct labor rate in your costing system

Update the rate from Step 2 in your cost system as your labor rate to be applied to products. Direct labor for any part is equal to

$$\text{Direct labor rate} \times \text{cycle time} \times \text{number of operators}$$

Update product cost by recalculating your standard cost. If you have updated your material cost based on most recent price paid, the cost system will now contain material cost by product (using last price paid times standard quantities required) and direct labor cost by product (using actual rate times standard labor hours required). There is no over/under absorption, because costs are at actual. Product in stock, whether WIP or finished goods, will carry a direct labor component based on current payroll costs and direct labor hours as specified in the BOM.

Step 4: Book inventory journal entry

Run an inventory value report (quantity on hand times cost) which summarizes the value in your closing inventory by cost element. In other words, the amount of your inventory value that represents material in inventory, the value that represents labor in inventory, and the value that represents overhead in inventory. Compare this month's labor in

Account	Debit	Credit
Inventory	$5,000.00	
Labor in inventory (COGS)		$5,000.00
Record inventory change for labor content		

FIGURE 11.4
Journal entry to record labor in inventory.

inventory to last month's labor in inventory and book an entry for the change (or use a reversing entry and book the entire value as shown on the report).

If your labor in inventory has increased by $5000, your entry would appear as shown in Figure 11.4.

11.7 SIMPLIFY OVERHEAD

There is no good reason to capture overhead by item. We have already established that there is not a *rate* or allocation base that makes sense for overhead on a product level in a high-mix environment. Just change your overhead rates to zero and stop attempting to allocate overheads to products. For full absorption costing (for GAAP), record just one journal entry (per month or even per year) to recognize the total amount of overhead in inventory. How much easier could it be?

Because of the nature of fixed costs, and the unrealistic idea that they can attach themselves to items, I recommend allowing actual costs be expensed as they are incurred. If your company is not publicly listed, just make the entry to record the change in overhead absorbed in your inventory at year end (overhead in this year's ending inventory minus overhead in last year's ending inventory). If you are required to report inventory at a full absorption cost on monthly financial statements, book the change entry to absorb inventory each month end.

And, while this does not eliminate the problem that fully absorbed costs motivate growing inventory, it does prevent personnel from looking at fully absorbed item costs and making poor decisions based on the product cost, including overhead.

To determine how much fixed overhead to absorb into your finished goods and work in process inventory, use the truly variable cost of inventory to determine the appropriate amount of actual fixed costs to record in inventory. Remember, truly variable costs are either based on material content or material content plus labor content if you opted to continue to capture direct labor costs. The assumption is that overhead is incurred evenly over the month (or specified period of time). This is basically the same calculation an auditor would use to insure that your overhead component of inventory is adequate, so it should meet all audit tests. The calculation is as follows:

Step 1: Determine the days in stock

Using the ending inventory number that has been calculated for material and direct labor, the days in stock can be determined as follows: (This example assumes that inventory remains in stock less than 30 days.)

$$\text{Average daily consumption} = \text{material dollars} + \text{direct labor}$$
$$\text{dollars/days in month}$$
$$\text{Ending inventory/average daily consumption} = \text{days in stock.}$$

Example : You buy $80,000 of material

You pay $10,000 in direct labor costs

The inventory report (including material and direct labor only) is $30,000

$$\text{Inventory turns} = \frac{\$80,000 + \$10,000}{\$30,000} = 3$$

$$\text{Days in inventory} = \frac{30 \text{ days in the month}}{3} = 10 \text{ days}$$

Step 2: Determine the overhead rate per day

Take the overhead cost total from your accounting system for the period of time which corresponds to your finished goods days in stock. If your finished goods turn in 30 days or less, use the costs for the current month. If your finished goods turn in 30–60 days, use the costs for the last 2 months.

Account	Debit	Credit
Inventory	$2,000.00	
Overhead in inventory (COGS)		$2,000.00
Record inventory change for OH content		

FIGURE 11.5
Journal entry to record overhead in inventory.

Average daily consumption = overhead cost divided by days in stock

$$\text{Average daily consumption} = \frac{\$80,000 + \$10,000}{10} = \$3,000 \text{ per day}$$

Step 3: Determine change in overhead in inventory

Total overhead in inventory = overhead rate per day × days in stock

Example : $3,000 per day × 10 days in stock = $30,000 overhead
in inventory

If the overhead in inventory at the last calculation was $28,000, then the inventory change for overhead is $2,000.

Step 4: Book inventory journal entry

Book the change in overhead or use a reversing entry and book the entire value of overhead in inventory (Figure 11.5).

11.8 SAMPLE INVENTORY ENTRIES

The accounting method described is a hybrid of a period and a perpetual inventory system. The quantity of inventory is perpetually updated, but the dollar value is updated only periodically. For planning purposes, that is, material requirements and determining what to buy, only inventory quantities are required, not dollars of inventory.

Accounting for inventory values in this fashion meets audit tests. An auditor will compare actual expenses and perform test to confirm that the balances shown accurately represent the value of inventory. Since the calculations are based on actual costs (not standards), the inventory value will meet these tests.

Sample entries are shown in Figure 11.6.

Account	Debit	Credit
Raw material purchases		
Raw material purchases	$×	
Accounts payable		$×
Payroll		
Direct labor expense	$×	
Cash		$×
Overhead purchases		
Supplies, rent, and so on.	$×	
Accounts payable		$×
Sale of inventory		
Accounts receivable	$×	
Sales revenue		$×
Pay for purchases		
Accounts payable	$×	
Cash		$×
Receive payment for sales		
Cash	$×	
Accounts receivable		$×
Inventory adjustment—raw materials		
Raw material inventory	$×	
Raw material purchases		$×
If this entry is a reversing entry, then book the total amount of raw materials in finished goods inventory at month end. If this entry is not booked as a reversing entry, this entry is for the net change.		
Inventory adjustment—finished goods		
Finished goods inventory	$×	
Raw material in inventory (COGS)		$×
Labor in inventory (COGS)		$×
OH in inventory (COGS)		$×
If this entry is a reversing entry, then book the total finished goods inventory at month end. If this entry is not booked as a reversing entry, this entry is for the net change.		

FIGURE 11.6
Sample journal entries.

12

Time-Based Metrics

Time-Based Metrics—If you value your time, then why don't you put a value on time?????

Metrics should, first and foremost, encourage desired behavior. Metrics for cells need to focus on reducing time, space, and defects. The traditional metrics of asset utilization, labor efficiency, and burden absorption do *not* encourage desired behavior and in fact are counterproductive to lead time reduction. These metrics must be eliminated.

We also know that metrics are most effective when:

- There are not too many of them.
- They are simple and easy to understand.
- They measure improvement over time.
- They measure the process, not the people.
- They are visual.
- They are timely.

We also know that financial measures are a result of many actions, and as such, are not operable metrics. Metrics must measure the actions that drive the results. Measures that motivate lead time reduction and velocity will drive results which can be validated by contribution per hour of MCT.

For cell metrics and time-based accounting, we should ensure that whatever we measure motivates the following as key objectives:

- Responsiveness, that is, lead time reduction
- Velocity or throughput of orders
- Quality or minimal defects
- Continuous improvement
- Flexibility, or the ability to react quickly to demand variations

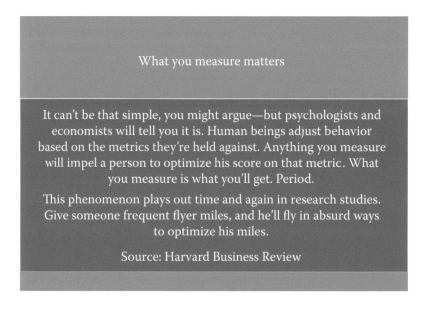

What you measure matters

It can't be that simple, you might argue—but psychologists and economists will tell you it is. Human beings adjust behavior based on the metrics they're held against. Anything you measure will impel a person to optimize his score on that metric. What you measure is what you'll get. Period.

This phenomenon plays out time and again in research studies. Give someone frequent flyer miles, and he'll fly in absurd ways to optimize his miles.

Source: Harvard Business Review

We will now look at some dysfunctional metrics and then focus on some more productive metrics for a time-based organization.

12.1 WHAT IS WRONG WITH UTILIZATION?

Utilization is a local measure, not a system measure. Utilization shows the percentage of time that a resource is utilized. For example, the most commonly used calculation of utilization divides run hours by available hours. Utilization does *not* show the percentage of time the resource *should* be used in order to achieve the shortest lead times. Maximizing the utilization of any one resource will not result in the shortest path through the system, in fact, quite the opposite.

Utilization, as a metric, implies that higher is better, with 100% representing *perfect* or total utilization. In fact, as resources get busy, wait times increase disproportionately. A portion of capacity (20%–25%) should always be reserved as a buffer for variability. The graph shown in Figure 12.1 is based on mathematical equations from queuing theory. When plotted on a graph, as utilization moves toward 100%, lead times rise disproportionately. There are plenty of examples from real life that illustrate the concept of queues in high utilization situations:

- The freeway at rush hour
- The lines in the supermarket at Thanksgiving or department stores at Christmas

Most ERP systems model utilization in a static model, without allowing for the variability of *real life*. This assumes that resources are available without consideration of the interaction between employees, materials, customers, and equipment. If one person is responsible for setup on five machines, and all five machines finish their jobs at the same time, how is that handled? If three people call in sick, is there allowance for this? How about when the customer has a large rush order? What if a critical piece of equipment goes down unexpectedly? What if a material problem causes an inordinate amount of scrap? These are all examples of variability that happens on a daily basis, but which are not factored into a static model. Therefore, not only is 100% utilization an unrealistic target, but it is also an unproductive target because there is no room for variability and real-life results will be worse than predicted, not better.

Figure 12.1 illustrates the lead time phenomena that occur as utilization approaches 100%.

Therefore, attaining or nearing the goal of 100% will increase lead time and reduce throughput rather than improving the ability to respond to customer needs.

In fact, the rapid growth of lead time that occurs as we move toward the right on the utilization graph can be quantified as the *magnifying effect of utilization* which is represented by *M* in the following formula:

$$M = \frac{\text{Utilization}(U)}{1 - \text{utilization}(U)}$$

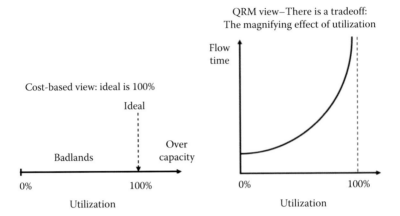

FIGURE 12.1

The relationship between utilization and lead time. (Reprinted from Suri, R., *It's About Time: The Competitive Advantage of Quick Response Manufacturing*, CRC Press, New York, 2010, p. 80. With permission.)

In other words, at 50% utilization, if the queue time is 2 h; then at 90% utilization the lead time will grow by a factor of $0.90/(1 - 0.90) = 9$ times, or 18 h! Does your ERP system adjust the schedule based on utilization? If not, as utilization reaches the upper ends, the system-generated schedule will be less and less attainable.

Do not forget that spare capacity applies to all resources, labor, as well as equipment. In either case, as resources approach 100% utilization, wait times increase and so does lead time. As labor utilization increases, so does the time spent waiting for labor. As equipment utilization increases, the time spent waiting for equipment also increases. The goal is not 100% machine utilization, nor is it 100% labor utilization. The goal is to apply resources in the best way to satisfy the customer, make money, and collect cash.

Utilization, when used as part of an evaluation to understand why systems behave the way they do, can provide valuable information. Utilization, when used as a performance metric, motivates increasing the number while ignoring the impact on other parts of the system.

12.2 WHAT IS WRONG WITH EFFICIENCY?

Efficiency, also a local measure, evaluates how a resource performs against an arbitrary standard. The most common efficiency measure is labor efficiency, although efficiency measures are often used for both machines (running faster or slower than planned) and people (performing processes faster or slower than planned). Labor efficiency is based on standard hours divided by actual hours. If standards dictate 8 h of labor for a particular product, and it takes 10 h, then you are 8/10 = 80% efficient. Efficiency measures are the product of assembly line time studies for repetitive processes. Manufacturing firms spend enormous amounts of time and effort on data collection systems for workers to clock in and out of jobs just to evaluate and report on labor efficiency. Since in most modern manufacturing operations direct labor comprises 10% (or less) of total cost, might we be spending time measuring something that will have a larger impact?

When used as a metric, higher efficiency is better. If we can match standard, we achieve 100% efficiency. There are two problems with the goal. First, 100% of what? How was the *standard* determined? Second, as all of our operators approach 100% utilization, we also experience the dysfunctional effect described earlier. If all operators achieved 100% efficiency, what would this look like? Would product magically flow, unimpeded, through the facility? Of course not. Since not all processes run at the same speed, nor do they require the same amount of labor, 100% labor efficiency will result in creating bottlenecks and WIP. Labor standards are rarely set with any assumption for the impact of utilization and mix. Labor standards do not assume that the operator may have to wait for a machine in order to complete the process; they only assume the amount of time required once the operator begins work on the part.

Efficiency measures are local measures. This means that they measure the efficiency of one specific process or operation. What they do not measure is the efficiency of the system. Nor do they take into account the interaction of people and machines. If you have one operator covering four machines, should they be expected to be 100% efficient at each machine? What are the odds that the operator will be available at precisely the time they need to perform the process at each machine?

Consider the following example which compares Company "A" and Company "B." Company A is production driven and seeks to maximize utilization and efficiency. Company B is customer driven and seeks to produce to order and meet customer demand. Company A produces to capacity with an equal volume each month. This results in inventory of $250,000 at the end of month 1 and month 2, which is consumed in month 3 (Figure 12.2).

Company A	Month 1 ($)	Month 2 ($)	Month 3 ($)	Total ($)
Production-material 65% cost	812,500	812,500	812,500	2,437,500
Production–DL 15% cost	187,500	187,500	187,500	562,500
Production–OH 20% cost	250,000	250,000	250,000	750,000
Total cost	1,250,000	1,250,000	1,250,000	3,750,000
Sales at cost	1,000,000	1,250,000	1,500,000	3,750,000
Inventory	250,000	250,000	—	—
Revenue at 50% markup	1,500,000	1,875,000	2,250,000	5,625,000
Cost	1,000,000	1,250,000	1,500,000	3,750,000
Gross profit	500,000	625,000	750,000	1,875,000

FIGURE 12.2
Production (utilization) driven.

Company B has the exact same volume and cost structure but produces to order with no inventory, as shown in Figure 12.3.

The gross profit margin appears to be exactly the same. However, Company A has invested resources in inventory, including the cash to buy raw materials, the costs associated with holding inventory, and transaction costs. This example assumes that the inventory is saleable and that the manufacturer is able to predict exactly what to make with no danger of forecast error or obsolescence. This is highly suspect and also highly unlikely. The profit margins *appear* to be the same because of the application of the matching principle. The costs associated with overproduction are stored away in inventory, to be realized when (or if) the inventory actually sells.

At the net profit level, the results are *not* the same. Company B benefits from improved cash flow and lower inventory holding and handling costs.

Company B	Month 1 ($)	Month 2 ($)	Month 3 ($)	Total ($)
Production–material 65% cost	650,000	812,500	975,000	2,437,500
Production–DL 15% cost	150,000	187,500	225,000	562,500
Production–OH 20% cost	200,000	250,000	300,000	750,000
Total cost	1,000,000	1,250,000	1,500,000	3,750,000
Sales at cost	1,000,000	1,250,000	1,500,000	3,750,000
Inventory	—	—	—	—
Revenue at 50% markup	1,500,000	1,875,000	2,250,000	5,625,000
Cost	1,000,000	1,250,000	1,500,000	3,750,000
Gross profit	500,000	625,000	750,000	1,875,000

FIGURE 12.3
Customer and lead time driven.

However, if the production metrics for Company B are based on utilization and efficiency, they will fail miserably compared to Company A in periods of lower demand. In periods of lower demand, the utilization and efficiency suffer at Company B because they are not putting inventory on the shelf in order to consume capacity.

What are the employees of Company B doing while the production levels are down based on demand? The return on having employees involved in cross-training and improvement projects (that may enable them to adjust to peak demand situations) far exceeds gains from putting product in inventory.

The examples illustrate that high utilization and high efficiency do not automatically correlate with higher profits. Production metrics must be consistent with company strategy. Companies that have a lead-time-focused strategy with a make-to-order model cannot demand high utilization and high efficiency and also expect production to be matched to demand at the same time.

12.3 HOW ABOUT OVERALL EQUIPMENT EFFECTIVENESS (OEE)?

OEE has received a lot of press, being hyped as the granddaddy of all metrics for operations managers. The behaviors and outcomes generated by using this metric are suboptimal because the measure is related to equipment, not the production system. The measure also does not take into account the interaction between people and machines and how that impacts lead time.

To understand this, let us look at the components of the measurement, and evaluate what behaviors and results the use of the OEE metric is likely to encourage:

$$OEE = \text{Machine utilization} * \text{performance} * \text{quality}$$

Utilization = production hours/total available, that is, 4 h out of 8 = 50% (Some variations substitute *availability* for utilization, which is the percentage of scheduled time that is actually available. This calculation moves the measure away from maximizing equipment usage toward minimizing down-time.)

Performance (efficiency) = standard cycle time/actual cycle time, that is, 90 cycles out of standard cycle of 100 = 90%

Quality = good parts produced out of total parts produced, that is, 95 parts out of 100 = 95%.

The OEE in this example = 50% * 90% * 95% = 42.75%

A production manager that was measured against OEE would have the following incentives:

- Keep machines running; whether the schedule is driven by demand or the production is going into stock.
- Run large batches to minimize change over time and maximize utilization.
- Run as many cycles as possible, as quickly as possible.
- Limit the number of rejects; regardless of cost—since the measure is on a unit basis, not a dollar basis. There is also a motivation to move questionable parts out the door, since there is no external reject (complaint) factor.

The metric is suboptimal because it optimizes machines; while ignoring optimization of the *system* or *process*. Only optimization of the system results in reducing overall process time by improving process flow, eliminating bottlenecks, and allowing demand to pull product through the system.

12.4 METRICS FOR TIME-BASED SYSTEMS

Imagine that you are a production manager and you are told that you need to reduce lead time, increase inventory turns, maximize equipment utilization, and minimize direct labor content. Where do you start? How can you possibly achieve these conflicting goals? If you focus on maximizing equipment utilization, you will increase lead time and reduce inventory turns. If you focus on minimizing direct labor content, you may jeopardize on-time deliveries. If you focus on lead time and inventory turns, you will most likely lower equipment utilization and labor efficiency. And yet, operations managers are put in this no-win situation every day!

Objective	Measure
Responsiveness, i.e., lead time reduction	MCT and/or QRM number
Velocity of throughput of orders	Contribution per day of MCT
Quality	Hours lost due to quality problems
Continuous improvement	Time saved with improvements
Flexibility	Skills cross-training % of ideal

FIGURE 12.4
Time based objectives and measures.

To reiterate, for cell metrics and time-based accounting, consider the five key measures shown in Figure 12.4.

Some suggestions for measurements and presentation of these key objectives follow.

12.4.1 Responsiveness: production lead time, QRM number

The definition of MCT, or M̲anufacturing C̲ritical Path T̲ime, as described in *It's About Time*, is very precise. The scope of the metric covers the *typical amount of calendar time from when a customer submits an order, through the critical-path, until the first end-item of that order is delivered to the customer.* For the metrics discussed as follows, the focus is on the portion of lead time which is under the control of the cell. The assumption is that a master scheduler (within or outside the cell) is authorizing a work order for production. This starts the clock for what is referred to as *Production MCT,* which is a subset of total MCT. The concepts of subsets of Total MCT, as well as the ability to drill down on segments of MCT time, are valid and can even be applied within the Production MCT Number. For example, the activity of setup or changeover might be one segment within Production MCT. Drilling down on the activity of changeover to identify gray space and white space might provide insights as to what causes waiting in the changeover process and which activities in changeover are on the critical path.

Although the metrics and focus of the majority of this book are specifically on manufacturing, MCT and QRM concepts can be applied throughout the business. White space is not limited to the production floor!

For those who like upward trends on line graphs to indicate improvement, Suri has proposed the QRM number which is calculated as:

$$\text{Current QRM number} = \frac{\text{Base period MCT}}{\text{Current period MCT}} \times 100$$

Not only does this have the advantage of showing a reduction in lead time as an upward trend, but it also recognizes improvements as a relative number rather than absolute which is a good motivator for continuous improvement.

The concept of the production MCT metric can be restated as a QRM number in the same fashion:

$$\text{Current production MCT number} = \frac{\text{Base period production MCT}}{\text{Current period production MCT}} \times 100$$

If you started with a 21-day production lead time, and you have reduced this by 4–17 days, the Production MCT Number is 124 (representing a 24% improvement):

$$124 = \frac{21}{17} \times 100$$

A sample graph for posting on the production floor is shown in Figure 12.5.

	Week 1	Week 2	Week 3	Week 4	Week 5	Week 6	Week 7	Week 8	Week 9
Prod MCT	30	25	24	32	30	22	20	18	17
QRM number	100.0	120.0	125.0	93.8	100.0	136.4	150.0	166.7	176.5

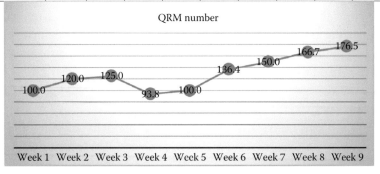

FIGURE 12.5
QRM number.

12.4.2 Quality: internal cost in hours

Although cost of quality can be calculated many ways, none of the popular methods properly include the cost of *time*. All are cost-based formulas that accumulate the cost in material and labor for scrap, rework, and inspection. Since all of these activities take time, which will add to lead time, why not calculate the cost of quality in time (hours)? Cost of quality in time would include the following:

- *Scrap hours*: How much time (run time) was spent making scrap?
- *Remake hours*: How much time was spent making good parts to replace defective parts?
- *Rework hours*: How much time was spent reworking defective parts?
- *Inspection hours*: How much time was spent in inspecting parts for quality?
- *Opportunity hours*: Without the scrap, how much time could we have spent making parts for another customer order?

Tracking and accumulating these hours (by cell) and extending the hours by the average contribution per hour—result in a *time-based* cost of quality. The result is the opportunity cost of quality; what could have been contributed to the bottom line had the same time been used to run good parts? This opportunity cost focuses on internal quality.

External quality is measured by DPPM (defective parts per million or the defective parts rejected or scrapped by the customer for every million parts produced). External DPPM involves the customer and cannot be neglected due to the very real and dangerous threat of customer dissatisfaction and interrupted production schedules. External DPPM is a high-level metric. However, external DPPM is really just internal scrap that got out the door. If we reduce the cost of quality (in hours), we will reduce scrap and minimize the probability of defective parts getting to our customer.

Quality data can be presented similar to the QRM number, by expressing improvement relative to the base period in the formula:

$$\text{Current quality number} = \frac{\text{Base period cost of quality hours}}{\text{Current period cost of quality hours}} \times 100$$

	Week 1	Week 2	Week 3	Week 4	Week 5	Week 6	Week 7	Week 8	Week 9
Scrap	10	7	12	6	8	8	12	15	5
Remake	10	7	12	6	8	8	12	15	5
Rework	15	0	5	9	8	5	15	10	6
Inspection	30	50	40	40	25	30	30	40	35
Total hours	65	64	69	61	49	51	69	80	51
Quality number	100.00	101.56	94.20	106.56	132.65	127.45	94.20	81.25	127.45

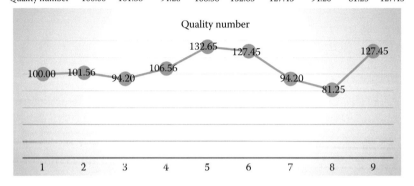

FIGURE 12.6
Quality number.

	Week 1	Week 2	Week 3	Week 4	Week 5	Week 6	Week 7	Week 8	Week 9
Scrap	10	7	12	6	8	8	12	15	5
Remake	10	7	12	6	8	8	12	15	5
Rework	15	0	5	9	8	5	15	10	6
Inspection	30	50	40	40	25	30	30	40	35
Total hours	65	64	69	61	49	51	69	80	51
Cont. $ per hour	$50	$50	$50	$50	$50	$50	$50	$50	$50
Weekly cost	$3250	$3200	$3450	$3050	$2450	$2550	$3450	$4000	$2550

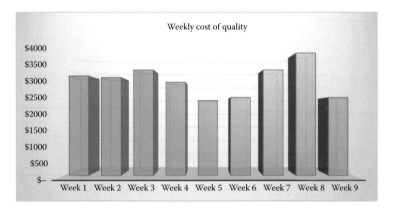

FIGURE 12.7
Time-based cost of quality.

Refer to Figure 12.6 for a calculation of the quality number metric.

Another presentation of the same quality data uses dollars in lieu of hours, showing the cost of quality in dollars by week. Expressing hours lost to quality issues as dollars has the added impact of tying the lost time to lost contribution in dollars. If the cell is tracking contribution per day of MCT, the dollar impact helps draw the correlation between the quality metric and the contribution metric (Figure 12.7).

12.4.3 Velocity number

Velocity number and incremental contribution: As first introduced in Chapter 8, this metric shows the bottom-line improvement of reducing lead times and improving throughput. This measures the incremental contribution (highlighted values on Figure 12.8) generated by

		Cell A	Cell B	Cell C	Total
A	Revenue	$100,000	$250,000	$175,000	$525,000
B	Variable cost	$35,000	$100,000	$135,000	$270,000
C = A − B	Contribution	$65,000	$150,000	$40,000	$255,000
D	Production hours	1,800	2,000	1,500	5,300
E = C/D	Contribution/production hour	$36.11	$75.00	$26.67	$48.11
F	Cumulative MCT days	100	250	175	525
G = C/F	Contribution/day of MCT	$650	$600	$229	$486
H = G/24	Contribution/hour of MCT	$27.08	$25.00	$9.52	$20.24
I = F*24	Total MCT (h)	2,400	6,000	4,200	12,600
J	Baseline cumulative MCT (h)	3,000	6,000	5,200	14,200
K	Baseline contribution	$65,000	$135,000	$30,000	$230,000
L = K/J	Baseline contribution/MCT hour	$21.67	$22.50	$5.77	$16.20
M = H − L	Incremental contribution/MCT hour	$5.42	$2.50	$3.75	$4.04
N = M*I	Incremental contribution	**$13,000**	**$15,000**	**$15,769**	**$50,915**
O = L*I	Check: if no change in rate	$52,000	$135,000	$24,231	$204,085
		$65,000	$150,000	$40,000	$255,000

FIGURE 12.8
Velocity and incremental contribution.

		Week 1	Week 2	Week 3	Week 4	Week 5
A	Revenue	$100,000	$125,000	$120,000	$90,000	$75,000
B	Variable cost	$35,000	$50,000	$45,000	$30,000	$25,000
C = A − B	Contribution	$65,000	$75,000	$75,000	$60,000	$50,000
D	Cumulative MCT days	100	120	110	90	75
E	Cumulative MCT hours	2,400	2,880	2,640	2,160	1,800
F	Contribution/hour of MCT	$27.08	$26.04	$28.41	$27.78	$27.78
G	Baseline contribution/ hour of MCT	$26.50	$26.50	$26.50	$26.50	$26.50
H = F/G*100	Velocity number (%)	102	98	107	105	105
K	Incremental contribution/ MCT hour	$0.58	$(0.46)	$1.91	$1.28	$1.28

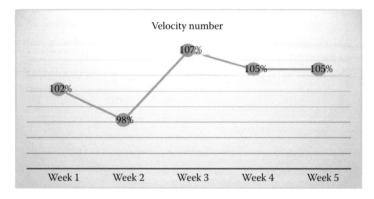

FIGURE 12.9
Velocity number.

velocity—additional throughput in the same lead time. This measure puts a dollar value to time and shows clearly how time translates to money (Figure 12.8).

Taking data for Cell A as representing 1 week of results, the results of the cell by week could be recorded and plotted. The Velocity Number tracks the improvement in Contribution per Hour of MCT as a percentage of the baseline (Figure 12.9).

12.4.4 Continuous improvement metrics: tracking CI projects in hours

This metric accumulates the white space reduction that occurs as a result of improvement projects.

Examples of projects in this category and the resulting calculations of results are as follows:

- Change over reduction: If average changeovers are reduced from 4 to 2 h, and the cell does 25 changes per week, the annual savings is 25 × 2 × 50 weeks = 2500 h.
- Downtime: If a preventive maintenance program is implemented that reduces equipment downtime by 2 h per week on each of three machines, the annual savings is 2 × 3 × 50 = 300 h.
- Supplies stored at point of use: If the move of supplies or materials into the cell saves 25 trips per week at 10 min each, the annual savings is 25 × 10/60 × 50 = 208 h.

One visual display option for the metric is to keep a running total for the year on a thermometer display (we are getting hot!) that accumulates hours from continuous improvement initiatives (Figure 12.10).

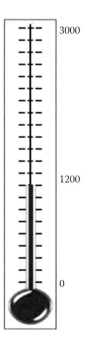

FIGURE 12.10
Hours saved by continuous improvement projects this year.

12.4.5 Cross-training matrix and metric

Cross-training creates a flexible work force that can flow to bottlenecks, which change from day to day in a high-mix, low-volume environment. Since a flexible and cross-trained work force will help achieve lead time reductions and/or improve the ability to respond to demand fluctuations, measuring the status of cross-training is a worthwhile exercise. The cross-training matrix shown in Figure 12.11 shows the number of individuals in a cell that are certified for each skill that has been defined as being required in the cell.

Note that what is being measured is not employees or positions; rather, it represents skills. The matrix shown is for five employees. Within the skill of *Machining,* ideally three team members would have this skill. Since only two employees currently qualify for the machining skill, there is a gap of one employee to be trained and certified in machining. All five team members are skilled in measuring; however, various team members each hold other subsets of skills. For any skill, there should be no fewer than two team members who are competent in that skill. With at least two, there is always a backup. The *ideal* number is based on the best mix of skills to minimize MCT. This is best analyzed with a planning tool that can properly analyze complex interactions between people and machines. In the absence of a tool to analyze these interactions, the team can provide insights based on their day-to-day experiences (why don't we ever have a machinist when we need one?) that will help establish the desired, or ideal, skill composition.

Skill	Assembly	Machining	Drilling	Measuring	Root cause analysis	Training	Total
Ideal	4	3	2	5	3	2	19
Actual	2	2	2	5	4	2	17
Gap	2	1	0	0	−1	0	2
Percent of ideal							89%

FIGURE 12.11
Sample skills matrix with % of ideal.

The metric, % of ideal, shows that while ideally our team of employees would have 19 skillsets, the current team has 17 skillsets, or 89% of ideal (17 of 19). Tracking this metric over time can illustrate progress toward cross-training objectives.

12.4.6 Linking cell metrics to financial results

Time based metrics have linkages to the bottom line. Refer to Figure 12.12 for a linkage diagram that links the five time based metrics we've discussed to financial measures.

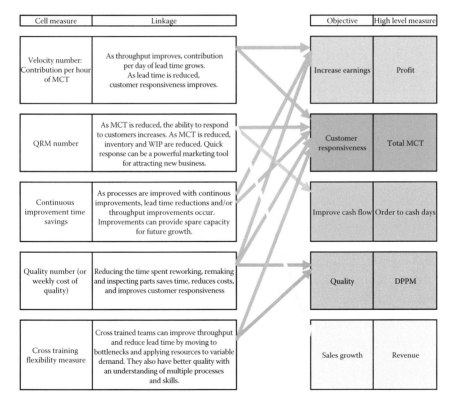

FIGURE 12.12
Linking time-based metrics to financial results.

Operational cell metrics should be graphed and posted on a weekly basis. High level metrics are best shown on a *scorecard* that is updated each month end. For scorecards, conditional highlighting for red/yellow/green scores helps the observer quickly note the successes (green) and the areas for improvement (red). A sample scorecard is shown in Figure 12.13.

Scorecard		Jan	Feb
Results	Earnings	$113k	$105k
	Contribution per hour of MCT	$25	$26
Revenue	Sales growth	2.50%	5.00%
Velocity	Order to cash	45	50
	Days FG inventory	10	15
	Days raw material inventory	50	55
Lead time	MCT - order to production	10	7
	MCT - production to ship	12	7
Continuous improvement	Time saved	40 h	15 h
Quality	Internal - hours making scrap, remaking, reworking, inspecting	60	45
	External defective parts per million	275	450
Cross trained, cross functional	Gap analysis (% ideal)	75%	80%

FIGURE 12.13
Time-based scorecard.

13

Time-Based Cost Justifications

Cost Justifications—How to show that time is a good investment.

The concept of lead time reduction, in combination with increased throughput, provides a basis to justify projects. The examples shown on the following pages illustrate how to show both types of savings to justify lead time reduction projects.

The *hard* dollars of traditional justification include labor savings, material savings, and reduction in operating expenses. These fall within the generally accepted cost categories of labor, material, and overhead. These categories are shown on the justification template under the headings of *Cell Time*, *Material*, and *Manufacturing Expenses*, with the hard dollars being calculated in the *$ Savings Column*. The *soft* dollars reflect the time saved with the project by taking time from the process and the potential value of the increased capacity. The payback is shown in two ways. First, the payback is shown with only "hard" dollars. Second, the payback is shown with both *hard* and *soft* dollars. The readiness of management to accept the *soft dollars* of incremental contribution potential with the creation of spare capacity depends on three factors:

- Whether lead time reduction is a competitive strategy for the organization

- Sales backlog and sales forecasts (can we sell into the new capacity?)
- How close to peak capacity the cell labor is at the moment, and the amount of demand variation they can handle (the difference between average and peak)

The templates shown in this chapter are based on projects for a manufacturing cell. Projects to eliminate white space from the office would use a different template (not included in this text). Examples would include elimination of time required for complex variance analysis in accounting, reducing the quoting lead time in engineering, fewer engineering change orders during the development process due to speed of development, procurement lead time savings with supply-chain initiatives, and so on.

13.1 SPARE CAPACITY PLANNING FOR EQUIPMENT

To justify spare capacity, calculate the lead time impact before and after the addition of equipment. The addition of equipment reduces lead time by reducing the time that a job waits for equipment to become available. The calculation requires formulas for lead time, utilization, and the effect of utilization on lead time (Suri, 1998, pp. 159–171). The formulas shown are derived from a branch of applied statistics called *queuing theory*.

1. *Calculate the current utilization*: Utilization is equal to the total time the equipment is occupied and unavailable for other work (Total Job Time or TJ) divided by the total time available (TA). Note that TJ is defined as all the time the work center is occupied and unavailable for another job. This includes setup, processing, take down, and repair. Example: If the equipment is occupied (as described) for 20 h a day out of 24, Utilization = 20/24 = 83%.
2. *Calculate the utilization after adding capacity*: Estimate the impact on utilization of adding capacity. For example, if adding another machine to the work center will cut utilization in half, the new utilization will be 10 h out of 24 or 42%.
3. *Calculate average queue time before and after the additional capacity*: Lead time is made up of the time the job is running plus the time that the job waits in queue. The queue time will increase or

decrease as utilization of the equipment increases or decreases. In order to estimate the impact of adding capacity, we need to understand how the additional equipment will impact queue time. In order to calculate Average Queue Time (QT), use the following formulas:

TJ = Mean time to process a job (including setup time and process time the entire lot). In other words, what is the average length of any job at this work center?

SJ = Standard deviation of time to process a job. In other words, how much variation is there in the length of time required to process the jobs at this work center?

TA = Mean time between arrivals of jobs to the work center. In other words, what is the average time between one job arriving to be processed and the next?

SA = Standard deviation of time between arrivals of jobs to the work center. In other words, how much variation is there in the arrival of jobs at the work center? Do they arrive regularly, in a steady stream? Or do they arrive in *peaks and valleys*?

VRA = Variability ratio for arrivals = SA/TA.

VRJ = Variability ratio for job times = SJ/TJ.

V = Variability = $VRA^2 + VRJ^2$.

M = Magnifying effect of utilization (M) = $U/(1 - U)$. We reviewed this formula earlier, which calculates the increase in both wait and lead times as the work center utilization nears capacity.

QT = Queue time = $(1/2) \times$ Variability*** (V) $\times$ magnifying effect of utilization (M) $\times$ average total job time (TJ).

While this may seem a bit daunting, a spreadsheet containing a representative group of work orders for a period of time can be used and formulas can do the math based on the raw data supplied (a sample of the spreadsheet can be viewed at Figure 13.11). To calculate standard deviation in job time (SJ) in our example, assume the following:

TJ = The average length of a job, from set up through tear down, is 10 h.

SJ = The standard deviation of time to process a job. Use the standard deviation formula for the jobs used in the average. For 10 jobs as shown with an average TJ of 20 h, the standard deviation (STDDEV) is 5.06 (Figure 13.1).

Job	TJ
1	8
2	10
3	12
4	6
5	2
6	20
7	10
8	11
9	6
10	15
Average	10
Standard deviation	5.06

FIGURE 13.1
Standard deviation (variability) of job times.

SA = Standard deviation of time between arrivals at the work center. SA is a bit trickier and may or may not be available in your system. The options for SA are as follows:

- Look at data when jobs are released (release date) to the shop floor for jobs destined for this resource and use the time between these job releases, assuming that arrivals have a similar pattern to job releases.
- If jobs are closely related to customer orders, then look at arrival patterns for customer orders for the relevant jobs (order date).
- Use manual observations for a period of time, such as a week.
- As a last resort use a value of 1.0 for arrival variability.

For our example, we will use release date of the work orders. The spreadsheet in Figure 13.2 calculates the standard deviation for arrivals as 4.96.

We now have the information we need to calculate Queue Time (QT).

VRA = Variability ratio for arrivals = SA 4.96/TA 5.28 = 0.94
VRJ = Variability ratio for job times = SJ 5.06/TJ 10 =0.51
V = Variability = $VRA^2 + VRJ^2$ = $0.94^2 + 0.51^2$ = 0.88 + 0.26 = 1.14
M = Magnifying Effect of Utilization (M) *Before* = 0.83/(1 − 0.83) = 4.88
M = Magnifying Effect of Utilization (M) *After* = 0.42/(1 − 0.42) = 0.72
QT = (1/2) × Variability (V) × Magnifying Effect of Utilization (M) × Average Total Job Time (TJ)

Job	Total job time (TJ) (h)	Release date	Arrival interval (h)
1	8	8/1/14; 10:00 AM	
2	10	8/1/14; 11:00 AM	1
3	12	8/1/14; 5:00 PM	6
4	6	8/1/14; 10:00 PM	5
5	2	8/2/14; 8:00 AM	10
6	20	8/2/14; 12:00 PM	4
7	10	8/2/14; 3:00 PM	3
8	11	8/2/14; 5:00 PM	2
9	6	8/3/14; 9:00 AM	16
10	15	8/3/14; 9:30 AM	0.5
Average	10	Average	5.28
Standard deviation	5.06	Standard deviation	4.96

FIGURE 13.2
Standard deviation (variability) of job arrivals.

QT *Before* = (1/2) × 1.14 × 4.88 × 10 = 27.8
QT *After* = (1/2) × 1.14 ×0.72 × 10 = 4.1

4. *Calculate the effect of utilization on lead time*: The estimated lead time impact of the additional equipment is 27.8 (before) minus 4.1 (after) = 23.7 h or a 1 day reduction.

The 1-day reduction in lead time is realized by reducing the time work spends in queue waiting for equipment. Even though the equipment is not fully utilized at 83%, jobs still wait an average of 28 h because of the variability in arrival times as well as the variability in average job duration. Although at face value purchasing equipment that will be used 42% of the time may seem like a poor investment, the knowledge that lead time can be reduced by 1 day may justify the time the equipment is idle. What is a day of lead time worth? If your current (and potential) customers value lead time, it can be worth a lot. Financially, this will cut inventory generated by this work center by 1 day, and this can be used in the justification. If the average output of the work center is $100,000 per day, and inventory generated from this work center takes 10 days to work through the system and ship, the work center is generating $1,000,000 average inventory. If this is cut to 9 days, the average inventory from the work center will be $900,000; a reduction of $100,000 (or 10%) on average. At a minimum, the inventory savings can be used for justification.

The reduction of inventory has a far greater impact than simply carrying costs. On the template, the savings associated with inventory include the following:

- *Transaction costs*: The transaction log from your inventory system can be used to estimate the reduction in transactions. Summarize the number of transaction recorded for adjustments, cycle counts, and inventory moves. Estimate the time required for each transaction, and be sure to include travel time, which is the time required to travel to and from a data entry device or station to record the transaction. For a 10% reduction in inventory, determine the transactions costs to be eliminated by multiplying the estimated total for the year by the 10% reduction. If there are 10,000 transactions per year, and each transaction takes 2 min, the time saved would be 10,000 * 2 * 10% = 2000 min or 33 h per year. This number can be multiplied by the direct labor rate (including benefits) to determine the savings in dollars, for example 33 h * $22.50 per hour = $742.50 per year. From an accounting perspective, there will be a question whether these savings are "real." Will we really eliminate 33 h of direct labor? Are we going to fire people? The answer is that you have freed up 33 h to either work on something else, cross train, or work on continuous improvement projects. The numbers are real, but often disputed and require nontraditional thinking about cells, labor, and saving time.
- *Expediting and rescheduling costs*: Keep a log of the number of expedited orders in any month. The best place to do this is in your scheduling or customer service area. Armed with this data, the number of expedites per year can be estimated. Reducing lead time *will* reduce expedites. Although the correlation may not be direct, a ballpark estimate is the lead time reduction (1 day out of 10 = 10%) times the number of expedites. Expediting costs typically take a considerable amount of time, including time in planning meetings, time to contact and negotiate with the customer, and time to update the order data in the system and reschedule. If there are 20 expedited per month, there are 240 per year. If we save 10%, we eliminate 24 per year. If each expedite takes 5 h, we have saved 120 h per year. This would typically be done by indirect labor; a savings estimate would be 120 h at $35 per hour = $4200 per year. (Again, are we going to fire our expeditors? Perhaps they could be redeployed to work at tasks and in

project that contribute more value.) Reduced expediting should also have a savings in the air/overnight freight costs in the Manufacturing Expenses section.

- *Opportunity cost*: The cost of holding inventory is much, much more than just interest. The fact that parts are being made to sit in stock (rather than shipping) implies that resources have been consumed to make these parts that could have been applied elsewhere. Therefore, the cost of capital (expected return on resource investments) is a better estimate of holding costs than an interest rate. It is not just about the tie-up of money; it is also about where else the money might have been used, as well as the missed revenue and associated profits from being too slow to capitalize on new opportunities. Multiply the opportunity cost times the average dollar reduction in inventory.

- *Warehouse space*: Estimate the space reduction and apply a rate per square foot. For rental buildings, use the rental rate. For owned buildings, use local rental rates to reflect the savings of not having to acquire additional space. Determine the space to be saved by taking the percentage of inventory to be eliminated times estimated storage space for the current inventory to determine square foot savings. Multiply square foot savings by the rate per square foot.

- *Obsolescence*: If you carry less inventory, you face a lower exposure to potential obsolescence. If your business has a high obsolescence rate, estimate the impact based on historical rates applied to the estimated inventory reduction.

Simulation or rapid modeling technology can be used to illustrate the impact of spare capacity on lead times.* The reduction in *waiting for equipment time* can be visually represented and help substantiate the lead time reduction recorded on the justification. In particular, Value Stream Modeling software is based on the same queuing theory formulas as those presented earlier to calculate wait times and lead times.

13.2 SPARE CAPACITY PLANNING FOR PEOPLE

Jobs can also wait for people. If you share operators among multiple pieces of equipment, there will be times when an operator is not available at the same time the equipment needs an operator. The incidence

---

* One example of rapid modeling software is Value Stream Modeling from Build to Demand, Inc.

will increase as the utilization of operators increase and as variability in demand and arrival times increase. Like equipment, the lead time calculation spreadsheet or dynamic modeling can illustrate the impact that adding personnel will have on queue time, based on the time spent waiting for operator(s). The utilization of an operator is similar to equipment. The utilization of an operator is represented by the time they are working on jobs compared to the total time they are available to work. No different than equipment, if your operators are utilized 100% there will be queues and delays. If *both* your equipment *and* your operators are at 100%, you will find yourself getting further and further behind. Even though traditional operation metrics present this as a desirable state, it produces very undesirable results!

On the justification template, adding labor to reduce lead time will be reflected by additional cost (labor and benefits) that are offset by lead time savings. Labor savings (in the form of automation) would be input on the justification as negatives. These carry through to dollars, but not hours. We cannot assume that saving labor means we will automatically save time. If we automate a process that replaces an operator, we have saved labor but we may or may not have saved time. If you have read *The Goal* by Eliyahu Goldratt you will remember the robot that created a pile of WIP at the next operation because the time saved was not on the critical path (at the bottleneck). The robot was very efficient, but the impact on the overall system was negligible. Care must be taken that labor savings that are based on the elimination of operators do not take the cell below the level required for optimal throughput, which is generated with spare capacity. Labor savings that relate specifically to time savings associated with reduced transaction volumes, reduced scrap, reduced changeovers, and reduced expediting are shown separately in the Cell Time section as a calculation based on hours.

13.3 TIME-BASED JUSTIFICATION TEMPLATE

The templates on the following pages incorporate both time and dollars. The payback on any project is calculated based on *hard* dollars and also by incorporating potential contribution.

Each illustration that follows is a tab from the justification spreadsheet:

Page 1/Tab 1 (Figure 13.3): Cover page and primary input page: Fields shaded in yellow are input fields. Fields shaded in orange represent financial data, as specified by your accounting group. Fields shaded in green are primary result fields. Notice that this form shows both dollar savings and hour savings. Hyperlinks on this tab go to supporting pages/tabs 2–7.

Page 2/Tab 2 (Figure 13.4): Manufacturing cell time: This section captures both time and dollars. Entries in this section reflect head count proposals (up or down) under Labor. Time savings associated with inventory reduction programs are shown in the appropriate categories in terms of hours. Time savings associated with time saving proposals (like reduction of changeover time) are shown in this section as well.

Page 3/Tab 3 (Figure 13.5): Materials: This section captures inventory changes and the impact of those changes. Traditional analyses use a *carrying cost* for inventory. For the time-based analysis, the material portion of the inventory change is assessed at an opportunity cost. This represents the hurdle rate the company would use for evaluating an investment. Investing in inventories assumes that the resultant return on that investment is equal or greater than alternative uses of the capital. The time savings associated with lower inventories (counting and handling) are captured in the cell time section (Tab 2) of the form, and the savings required with reduced storage space are captured in the Manufacturing Expense section (Tab 4) of the form.

Page 4/Tab 4 (Figure 13.6): Manufacturing expenses: For recording operating expenses that are impacted by the project, such as operating supplies, utilities, or shipping.

Page 5/Tab 5 (Figure 13.7): One-time costs: The costs of implementing which include training, equipment purchases, and installation.

Page 6/Tab 6 (Figure 13.8): Financial data: The financial data should be updated by accounting/finance personnel for the cell. The data on this tab are linked to the calculations on the cover page.

Page 7/Tab 7 (Figure 13.9): Lead time calculations: The data on this page should be updated with actual work order data for a representative sample of work orders and a representative period of time—a week or a month.

COLOR KEY		INPUT FIELD	FINANCE TAB		RESULTS	
Use hyperlinks for further information, to add notes and assumptions. Enter savings as a positive, costs as a negative.						
Project Description - What Will be Done? How will it be different from today? Who Will Do It? How Long Will it Take?						
Annual Recurring Savings (Costs)						
Cell Time	Before	After	Units	$ Per Unit	$ Savings	Time Savings (hrs)
Supervision			Hours	$35.00	$ -	
Direct Labor			Hours	$22.50	$ -	
Overtime			Hours	$33.75	$ -	
Cycle Time			Hours	$22.50	$ -	-
Change Over Time			Hours	$22.50	$ -	-
Down Time			Hours	$22.50	$ -	-
Inspection			Hours	$22.50	$ -	-
Inventory Transactions (hours = (Tx count * minutes per Tx)/60)			Hours	$22.50	$ -	-
Inventory Counts			Hours	$22.50	$ -	-
Material Handling (travel time)			Hours	$22.50	$ -	-
Material Handling (Tx Time = (Tx count * minutes per Tx)/60)			Hours	$22.50	$ -	-
Rework Time			Hours	$22.50	$ -	
Scrap Time (* hour savings are doubled)			Hours	$22.50	$ -	-
Expediting and Schedule Changes			Hours	$35.00	$ -	-
Total Cell Savings - Direct Labor and TIME					$ -	-
Average Contribution Per Hour					$	50.00
Incremental ThroughPut Potential					$	-
Materials						
Purchases			Dollars	n/a	$ -	
Raw Material Inventory			Dollars	20%	$ -	
WIP Inventory			Dollars	20%	$ -	
Finished Goods Inventory			Dollars	20%	$ -	
Scrap Material Cost			Units	$2.75	$ -	
Rework Material Cost			Dollars	n/a	$ -	
Obsolescence			Dollars	n/a	$ -	
Material Savings	-	-			$ -	
Manufacturing Expenses						
Air Freight, Overnight Shipping			Dollars	n/a	$ -	
Floor Space			Sq Ft	$5.00	$ -	
Utilities			KWH	$0.04	$ -	
Operating Supplies			Dollars	n/a	$ -	
Manufacturing Expense Savings					$ -	
Total Annual Savings					$ -	
One Time Costs to Implement						
One Time Costs						
Equipment or Software			Dollars			
Training			Dollars			
Installation			Dollars			
Outside Services			Dollars			
Cost To Implement					$ -	
Payback in Years (Cost to Implement/Annual Savings)					#DIV/0!	
Payback in Years with Incremental Contribution (Cost to Implement / (Annual Savings + Incr. Contribution)					#DIV/0!	
Lead Time Reduction in Hours (from Lead Time Tab)					#DIV/0!	

FIGURE 13.3

Time-based cost justification—Tab 1—summary.

Cell Time
Notes, Comments, and Additional Information for Entries in the "Cell Time" Section
Labor
Lines shaded in gray are so shown because they represent gray space. Use this line for labor reductions only if labor will be moved out of the cell by the project, or if the project will postpone additional hires and this can be demonstrated by data. Examples of this category would be automation that would replace current operations in the cell. Projects that increase throughput with time savings should be recorded in cells below. Note that it could be possible to add labor (entered as a negative to reflect a COST not a savings) that would pay for itself by reducing overall lead time and increasing throughput as shown on subsequent lines. Record hours of labor before and after the project. If overtime is part of the justification, do not include overtime hours here; rather use the next line. Hours should be stated on an annual basis.
Overtime
This category should be used for projects that will reduce or eliminate overtime. Record the annual number of hours of overtime before the project and after the project. Note that the rate is automatically adjusted for time and a half.
Cycle Time
Record changes that reduce the cycle time for any part. Use the number of parts per year times cycle time before and after for entry of hours before and after.
Change Over Time
Record change over time reductions. Record the difference between the last part before the change and the first part after the change. Multiple the before and after times by the number of changes per year that will be affected.
Inspection
Record annual inspection time required before and after the project. Inspection time can be impacted by process improvements and sequence of processing, new inspection equipment, or equipment that eliminates potential defects.
Inventory Transactions
This category includes any changes that reduce the number of inventory transactions required. Most typical is the reduction of inventory itself; but other possibilities include system changes that automate the recording of transactions, like scanning. Use the average time per transaction times the number of transactions (annually) before and after the change. Be sure and convert to HOURS.
Inventory Counts
This category **always** applies to inventory reductions, and reflects the fact it takes less time to count inventory if you don't have as much. The time applies to both cycle count programs and physical counts. Use the number of transactions eliminated x the number of counts x the average time per transaction. Be sure and convert to HOURS.
Material Handling (travel)
Use this category for handling of raw materials, WIP, and supplies. Most common projects in this category are those to store supplies and materials in the cell at point of use. Another example would be reorganizing equipment to streamline the flow of product through the cell. Use the time saved per work order times number of work orders impacted by the change.
Material Handling (transactions)
This category is used for the transaction time associated with moving product from one location to another in the system. A project in this category would be to change the system to backflush materials directly from the cell location, eliminating the need to record transactions to move material to and from a staging location. Use the average time per transaction times Ihe number of transactions (annually) before and after the
Rework Time
Record the change in rework time as a result of this projecct. Projects that impact inspection time (above) often impact rework time as well. Record the annual rework time before and after the change in hours.
Scrap Time (* hour savings are doubled)
Scrap has a double impact, because you not only waste the time to process the scrap, you have to replace the scrapped parts by remaking good ones. Hours recorded here are automatically doubled in the savings formula. Enter the time spent making scrap (scrap parts per year x average cycle time) before and after the change
Expediting and Schedule Changes
What is the impact on the cell for expedites and last minute changes? Do you have to break into another order, and if so, what is the break-in time? Is there a daily production planning meeting just for this purpose? How many people spend how much time in these meetings? Record the annual time impact of expedites, before and after the change.

FIGURE 13.4

Time-based cost justification—Tab 2—manufacturing cell time.

Materials
Notes, Comments, and Additional Information for Entries in the "Materials" Section
Purchases
This is for the material impact of the project, when it changes the cost of material purchases. A project to source locally vs overseas might cost more here (enter cost as a negative) but would reduce material travel time (above) and also freight in (below). Projects that involve the amount of purchases (reducing or increasing inventory) should be shown in the appropriate inventory section. Record the purchase dollars before and after the project.
Raw Material Inventory
Record the average inventory, before and after the change, in dollars. Raw material can frequently be reduced by supply chain initiatives that improve the response time of the supplier. Note that the financial impact is based on cost of capital or opportunity cost. Investing in inventory represents a decision to invest in this material instead of another material, or another opportunity in the business.
WIP Inventory
Record the average inventory, before and after the change, in dollars. WIP can often be eliminated by flattening bills of material and using a continuous process within a cellular manufacturiing structure. Note that the financial impact is based on cost of capital or opportunity cost. Investing in inventory represents a decision to invest in this material instead of another material.
Finished Goods Inventory
Record the average inventory, before and after the change, in dollars. Finished goods inventory can be reduced by shortening lead times, reducing lot sizes, and buildng to order. Inventory reductions should also accompanied by transaction time reductions in the Cell Time
Scrap Material Cost
This is for the material cost of scrap, before and after the project. Use an annual estimate of scrap units before and after the project. If you have an entry here, you should also have an entry in the cell time section to record the time associated with the scrap.
Rework Material Cost
This is for the material cost of rework, before and after the project. Rework involves salvaging some part of the product, but may require replacing components in addition to rework labor. Use an annual estimate of rework material costs before and after the project. If you have an entry here, you should also have an entry in the cell time section to record the time associated with the rework.
Obsolescence
Reduced inventories often result in lesser obsolescence. The less you keep, the less likely it is to go obsolete. If this project reduces inventory, consider whether it may also reduce exposure to obsolescence. Enter dollars before and after; a suggested calculation is to take the % obsolete before and estimate the % reduction based on the % of inventory reduction.

FIGURE 13.5

Time-based cost justification—Tab 3—materials.

Manufacturing Expenses
Notes, Comments, and Additional Information for Entries in the "Manufacturing Expenses" Section
Air Freight, Overnight Shipping
Enter expected dollars before and after the change. Reducing lead time often reduces the number of expedited shipments that require special freight (overnight or air).
Floor Space
This line item is for projects that affect the floor space required in the cell, or for storage of materials and inventory. Adding equipment in the cell may require additional floor space, which would increase requirements. Inventory reduction can reduce floor space requirements.
Utilities
This line item is for projects that affect utility expense. Most common in this area is the consumption of utilities required by a new machine in the cell.
Operating Supplies
Use this line for changes in operating supplies as a result of this project.

FIGURE 13.6

Time-based cost justification—Tab 4—manufacturing expenses.

One Time Costs
Notes, Comments, and Additional Information for Entries in the "Manufacturing Expenses" Section
Equipment or Software
This line for equipment (machines, computers, printers) to be purchased; also software programs.
Training
This line for training expenses associated with new processes, programs, equipment.
Installation
Include installation, freight, taxes; also any travel and lodging for installation personnel.
Outside Services
Outside services used for training, consulting, and set up of new program, process, or equipment.

FIGURE 13.7

Time-based cost justification—Tab 5—one time costs.

Cell Operations			
Supervisor	$35.00	per hr	Average hourly rate, including payroll tax and benefits
Direct Labor	$22.50	per hr	Average hourly rate, including payroll tax and benefits
Overtime	$33.75	per hr	Overtime rate (1.5) times average hourly rate
Average Contribution per Hour	$50.00	per hr	Annual: (Cell Revenue - Direct Costs) / Production (Gray space) hours
Materials			
Cost of Capital (Opportunity Cost)	20%		Not "carrying cost", but opportunity cost. The choice to invest dollars in inventory implies that those dollars have a better return than other potential uses of the funds
Warehouse Space	$5.00	per sq ft per year	Annual lease or rent / warehouse square footage. (may be same as manufacturing rate per square foot except when separate warehouse locations exist)
Average Unit Cost (Material & Labor)	$2.75		(Annual cell material + Annual cell direct labor) / Annual cell units
Manufacturing Expensess			
Utilities per KWH	$0.04	per kwh	From utility bills
Manufacturing Floor Space	$5.00	per sq ft per year	Annual lease or rent / square footage.

FIGURE 13.8

Time-based cost justification—Tab 6—financial data for calculations.

Utilization			Total Job Time (TJ)	Total Available Time (TU)	Utilization (U)
Current State					#DIV/0!
Future State					#DIV/0!
M (before)					#DIV/0!
M (after)					#DIV/0!
(A)	(B)	(C)	(D) = (B) + (C)	(E)	(F) = (E) This row minus (E) Last row*24
Job or Work Order Number	Setup Time (hours)	Run Time (hours)	Total Job Time (TJ) in Hours	Release Date (or Order Data) (SORT TABLE ON THIS COLUMN)	Arrival Interval (hrs)
			0		
			0		0
			0		0
			0		0
			0		0
			0		0
			0		0
			0		0
			0		0
Average TJ = AVERAGED(D)			0	Average TA = AVERAGE(F)	0.00
Std Dev SJ = STDEV(D)			0.00	Std Dev SA = STDEV(f)	0.00
VRJ = TJ/SJ			#DIV/0!	VRA = TA/SA	#DIV/0!
Variability = $VRJ^2 + VRA^2$			#DIV/0!		
QT Before (Hours)			#DIV/0!	QT After (Hours)	#DIV/0!
				Change in Hours	#DIV/0!
				Change in Days	#DIV/0!

For LEAD TIME REDUCTION, remember to estimate the following:

Inventory Reduction, determine % based on % reduction in lead time

Reduced inventory transactions related to fewer moves, fewer counts

Reduced storage space requirements

Reduced expediting and rescheduling time

Reduced air freight and expedited shipping

FIGURE 13.9
Time-based cost justification—Tab 7—lead time calculations.

13.4 TIME-BASED JUSTIFICATION EXAMPLES

Examples on the following pages include:

- A justification for equipment that will reduce setup and changeover time (Figure 13.10).

COLOR KEY		INPUT FIELD	FINANCE TAB		RESULTS	
— Use hyperlinks for further information and to add notes and assumptions. Enter savings as a positive, costs as a negative.						
Project Description - What Will be Done? How will it be different from today? Who Will Do It? How Long Will it Take?						
Procure magentic platen for press. Currently, it takes two operators 25 minutes to clamp the mold. The magnetic clamping system will reduce this to 5 minutes for one operator. There are 500 changes per year on this equipment, saving 20 minutes per change × 500 changes. The elimination of one operator per change is shown as a labor savings. The reduction in change time is shown as time savings per change. Lead time reduction is significant, as there is increased availability of the equipment as well as increased availability of operators.						
Annual Recurring Savings (Costs)						
Cell Time	Before	After	Units	$ Per Unit	$ Savings	Time Savings (hrs)
Supervision			Hours	$ 35.00	$ -	
Direct Labor	208	-	Hours	$ 22.50	$ 4,688	
Overtime			Hours	$ 33.75	$ -	
Cycle Time			Hours	$ 22.50	$ -	-
Change Over Time	208	42	Hours	$ 22.50	$ 3,750	167
Down Time			Hours	$ 22.50	$ -	-
Inspection			Hours	$ 22.50	$ -	-
Inventory Transactions (hours = (Tx count * minutes per Tx)/60)			Hours	$ 22.50	$ -	-
Inventory Counts			Hours	$ 22.50	$ -	-
Material Handling (travel time)			Hours	$ 22.50	$ -	-
Material Handling (Tx Time = (Tx count * minutes per Tx)/60)			Hours	$ 22.50	$ -	-
Rework Time			Hours	$ 22.50	$ -	-
Scrap Time (* hour savings are doubled)			Hours	$ 22.50	$ -	-
Expediting and Schedule Changes			Hours	$ 35.00	$ -	
Total Cell Savings - Direct Labor and TIME					$ 8,438	167
Average Contribution Per Hour						$ 50.00
Incremental ThroughPut Potential						$ 8,333
Materials						
Purchases			Dollars	n/a	$ -	
Raw Material Inventory			Dollars	20%	$ -	
WIP Inventory			Dollars	20%	$ -	
Finished Goods Inventory			Dollars	20%	$ -	
Scrap Material Cost			Units	$ 2.75	$ -	
Rework Material Cost			Dollars	n/a	$ -	
Obsolescence			Dollars	n/a	$ -	
Material Savings	-	-			$ -	
Manufacturing Expenses						
Air Freight, Overnight Shipping			Dollars	n/a	$ -	
Floor Space			Sq Ft	$ 5.00	$ -	
Utilities			KWH	$0.04	$ -	
Operating Supplies			Dollars	n/a	$ -	
Manufacturing Expense Savings					$ -	
Total Annual Savings					$ 8,437.50	
One Time Costs to Implement						
One Time Costs						
Equipment or Software			Dollars		$ (15,000)	
Training			Dollars			
Installation			Dollars			
Outside Services			Dollars			
Cost To Implement					$ (15,000)	
Payback in Years (Cost to Implement/Annual Savings)						1.78
(Incremental Contribution)						0.89
Lead Time Reduction in Hours (from Lead Time Tab)						−48

FIGURE 13.10
Example 1: Justify equipment.

- A justification for a process improvement that will reduce handling and travel times (Figure 13.11).

COLOR KEY		INPUT FIELD	FINANCE TAB		RESULTS	
Use hyperlinks for further information and to add notes and assumptions for any section. Enter savings as a positive, costs as a negative.						
Project Description - What Will be Done? How will it be different from today? Who Will Do It? How Long Will it Take?						
Storage for dies in the cell will save travel time and allow quicker pre-staging. With 5,000 changes per year and a reduction from 15 minutes to 5 minutes retrieval time, this saves 50,000 minutes per year or 833 hours. Used racks have been located at a cost of $15,000.						
Annual Recurring Savings (Costs)						
Cell Time	Before	After	Units	$ Per Unit	$ Savings	Time Savings (hrs)
Supervision			Hours	$ 35.00	$ -	
Direct Labor			Hours	$ 22.50	$ -	
Overtime			Hours	$ 33.75	$ -	
Cycle Time			Hours	$ 22.50	$ -	-
Change Over Time			Hours	$ 22.50	$ -	-
Down Time			Hours	$ 22.50	$ -	-
Inspection			Hours	$ 22.50	$ -	-
Inventory Transactions (hours = (Tx count * minutes per Tx)/60)			Hours	$ 22.50	$ -	-
Inventory Counts			Hours	$ 22.50	$ -	-
Material Handling (travel time)	1,250	417	Hours	$ 22.50	$ 18,750	833
Material Handling (Tx Time (Tx count * minutes per Tx)/60)			Hours	$ 22.50	$ -	-
Rework Time			Hours	$ 22.50	$ -	-
Scrap Time (* hour savings are doubled)			Hours	$ 22.50	$ -	-
Expediting and Schedule Changes			Hours	$ 35.00	$ -	-
Total Cell Savings - Direct Labor and TIME					$ 18,750	833
Average Contribution Per Hour						$ 50.00
			Incremental ThroughPut Potential			$ 41,667
Materials						
Purchases			Dollars	n/a	$ -	
Raw Material Inventory			Dollars	20%	$ -	
WIP Inventory			Dollars	20%	$ -	
Finished Goods Inventory			Dollars	20%	$ -	
Scrap Material Cost			Units	$ 2.75	$ -	
Rework Material Cost			Dollars	n/a	$ -	
Obsolescence			Dollars	n/a	$ -	
Material Savings	-	-			$ -	
Manufacturing Expenses						
Air Freight, Overnight Shipping			Dollars	n/a	$ -	
Floor Space			Sq Ft	$ 5.00	$ -	
Utilities			KWH	$ 0.04	$ -	
Operating Supplies			Dollars	n/a	$ -	
Manufacturing Expense Savings					$ -	
Total Annual Savings					$ 18,750.00	
One Time Costs to Implement						
One Time Costs						
Equipment or Software			Dollars		$ (15,000)	
Training			Dollars			
Installation			Dollars			
Outside Services			Dollars			
Cost To Implement					$ (15,000)	
Payback in Years (Cost to Implement/Annual Savings)						0.80
(Contribution)						0.25
Lead Time Reduction in Hours (from Lead Time Tab)						

FIGURE 13.11

Example 2: Process improvement—die storage at point of use.

- A justification for a project that will reduce batch sizes, add personnel for the added changes, and reduce overall lead times (Figure 13.12).

COLOR KEY		INPUT FIELD	FINANCE TAB		RESULTS	
Use hyperlinks for further information and to add notes and assumptions for any section. Enter savings as a positive, costs as a negative.						
Project Description - What Will be Done? How will it be different from today? Who Will Do It? How Long Will it Take?						
Analysis of actual work order data for past six months shows that lead time can be reduced by 14 days by reducing lot sizes and by adding additional operators for change-overs and cross-training. Set up time will be cut in half (from 2 hours to 1 hour), enabling more setups to be done for lower lot sizes in the same amount of time. The reduced lead time will reduce finished goods inventory by 50% and virtually eliminate work-in-process inventories.						

Annual Recurring Savings (Costs)						
Cell Time	Before	After	Units	$ Per Unit	$ Savings	Time Savings (hrs)
Supervision			Hours	$ 35.00	$ -	
Direct Labor	8,320	12,480	Hours	$ 22.50	$ (93,600)	
Overtime			Hours	$ 33.75	$ -	
Cycle Time			Hours	$ 22.50	$ -	
Change Over Time			Hours	$ 22.50	$ -	-
Down Time			Hours	$ 22.50	$ -	-
Inspection			Hours	$ 22.50	$ -	
Inventory Transactions (hours=(Tx count * minutes per Tx)/60)	1,000	500	Hours	$ 22.50	$ 11,250	500
Inventory Counts	333	167	Hours	$ 22.50	$ 3,735	166
Material Handling (travel time)			Hours	$ 22.50	$ -	-
Material Handling (Tx Time = (Tx count * minutes per Tx)/60)			Hours	$ 22.50	$ -	-
Rework Time			Hours	$ 22.50	$ -	-
Scrap Time (* hour savings are doubled)			Hours	$ 22.50	$ -	-
Expediting and Schedule Changes	475	0	Hours	$ 35.00	$ 33,250	475
Total Cell Savings - Direct Labor and TIME					$ (45,365)	1,141
Average Contribution Per Hour						$ 50.00
			Incremental ThroughPut Potential			$ 57,050
Materials						
Purchases			Dollars	n/a	$ -	
Raw Material Inventory			Dollars	20%	$ -	
WIP Inventory	150000	7500	Dollars	20%	$ 28,500	
Finished Goods Inventory	250000	125000	Dollars	20%	$ 25,000	
Scrap Material Cost	5000	2500	Units	$ 2.75	$ 6,875	
Rework Material Cost			Dollars	n/a	$ -	
Obsolescence			Dollars	n/a	$ -	
Material Savings	405,000	135,000			$ -	
Manufacturing Expenses						
Air Freight, Overnight Shipping	10000	5000	Dollars	n/a	$ -	
Floor Space	8000	4000	Sq Ft	$ 5.00	$ 20,000	
Utilities			KWH	$ 0.04	$ -	
Operating Supplies			Dollars	n/a	$ -	
Manufacturing Expense Savings					$ 20,000.00	
Total Annual Savings					$ 35,010.00	
One Time Costs to Implement						
One Time Costs						
Equipment or Software			Dollars			
Training			Dollars		$ (15,000)	
Installation			Dollars			
Outside Services			Dollars			
Cost To Implement					$ (15,000)	
Payback in Years (Cost to Implement/Annual Savings)						0.43
Payback in Years With Incremental Contribution (Cost to Implement / (Annual Savings + Incremental Contribution)						0.16
Lead Time Reduction in Hours (from Lead Time Tab)						336

FIGURE 13.12

Example 3: Justify additional personnel and lower batch sizes to reduce lead time.

14

A Road Map for Implementing Time-Based Accounting

 Time to get started.

1. *Read "It's About Time" and gain an understanding of the principles of Quick Response Manufacturing (QRM)*: To get a clear picture of the value of time from a customer and enterprise perspective, rather than simply an accounting perspective, read "It's About Time." If this strategy is one that will strengthen your business and ensure viability and growth, then have everyone in your business read the book and continue on to step two.

2. *Define your cells or value streams*: Carefully analyze your business to determine which products, processes, and equipment are best suited to a cellular structure. This will require relocating people and equipment. You cannot call something a *cell* without realigning reporting relationships and colocating resources. The cell must have control of their resources and therefore control of their results. Look for products that use similar resources (both people and equipment) and which have sufficient volume to support a cell. You do not have to do everything at once. You can start with one cell and grow the concept.

3. *Modify product costing. At a minimum, eliminate overhead absorption into product costs. Eliminate complex variance accounting and/or standard costing*: Fully absorbed product costs will hinder your efforts to implement this strategy. Turn off variance reporting

and set your overhead rates to zero. Whether you use standard or actual absorption of overhead, eliminate the absorption of overhead by product and record overhead in inventory with one entry. This accounting treatment (i.e., absorb overhead with one entry) can be used for both cellular and noncellular operations. The practice of allocating overheads and researching variances is nonvalue added, period. Remember that in a make-to-order environment with time as a metric, finished goods inventory will be minimal and production rates will be roughly equivalent to shipping rates. In this environment, the financial statement impact of inventory misstatement due to overhead or labor allocations is minimal, and in no way justifies the complicated methods required to achieve it. Use the last price paid as your *standard* cost of purchased materials. Use a journal entry to capitalize costs for the current month in total.

4. *Flatten bills of material*: Wherever possible, combine bills of material. In a cellular environment, eliminate subassembly (WIP) items and have one routing from start to finish. Try to have the same number of bills of material as end items. Reduce the number of transactions that have to be input by simplifying routings and also carefully analyze the cost/benefit of complex data collection requirements.

5. *Define variable cost*: Material is the only truly variable cost. Evaluate the importance and necessity, for your business, of including direct labor in product cost. If you choose to do this, use the total labor in the cell without regard for direct vs. indirect. If you choose not to do this, set labor rates to zero and treat similarly to overhead with one journal entry to capitalize labor.

6. *Develop feedback loops*: Make sure the cell has a way to provide feedback on actual vs. planned results for a product/work order/process. This is necessary to ensure that data used for capacity planning is accurate, as well as evaluating quoted vs. actual and taking corrective action as necessary to ensure profitability. Use feedback loops and/or random time studies in place of complex data collection methods that take cell personnel away from fulfilling orders and adding value.

7. *Define cell MCT*: Define the MCT calculation for the cell. What is under the control of the cell? What is the starting point (e.g., work order release or authorization) and what is the ending point

(e.g., work order completion and move to warehouse)? Will the units measured be minutes, hours, or days?

8. *Implement measurements for cell contribution*: For products produced in the cell, make sure you can collect and report revenue and variable costs. Above all, make sure you can measure and report cell lead time (MCT).

9. *Calculate base line*: Collect and track historical data on cell MCT and contribution. Baseline data will be used to determine improvements from baseline over time.

10. *Time-based scorecard*: Create a high-level snapshot view that shows both operational, strategic, and financial results. Color-code the scorecard for quick and easy analysis of problem areas.

11. *Time-based operating metrics*: Reevaluate your operational metrics and replace efficiency and utilization with time-based metrics. Consider the examples presented in this book (listed in the following) and adapt to your business as necessary. However, measuring lead time (MCT) is nonnegotiable. This is key to any time-based strategy. Examples of time-based metrics are as follows:
    a. Production MCT Time
    b. Velocity Number (Contribution per Hour of MCT)
    c. Quality—hours lost (scrap, rework, inspection) and DPPM
    d. Continuous Improvement (time saving projects)
    e. Cross-Training—% of Ideal

12. *Measure improvement*: Setting ambitious targets sometimes helps with quantum improvements and requires thinking in new ways. Caution should be exercised, as overly ambitious targets may also discourage and demotivate the cell. No matter what the target, measure improvements rather than simply measuring performance to target. This shows progress and helps keep the target from being a demotivator.

13. *Revise financial statements*: Simplify your financial statements and eliminate the standard cost-based reporting of variances in your financial statements. Use a value-added format and track variable costs by cell and overheads in total. Make it easy to see revenue, labor, and material costs without having to add and subtract variance accounts.

14. *Correlate pricing with time*: Evaluate your pricing model to ensure that it incorporates the concept of time. If you use gross profit to establish pricing, do an analysis to compare gross profit to contribution per

hour and think about how this may impact results. Think about how a change in price structures based on time would affect pricing in your market segments. Calculate a before and after price under each approach and consider what this tells you. Are some of what you believed to be the most profitable items suddenly not so attractive?

15. *Educate others*: Communicate, communicate, and communicate. Train, train, and train. Then communicate and train some more. There is no such thing as over communication. The mind-set change is significant and there will be resistance to change. The best way to combat this is with education, training, and demonstrating success.

15

Making Customers Wait…

In conclusion, here is a recap of how traditional accounting methods may be making your customers wait:

- By motivating long runs to amortize overhead and setup costs. Remember, there are customer orders waiting in queue behind the long run.
- By motivating large purchase quantities of raw materials to obtain discounts, but which result in large inventories. Cash invested in raw materials, especially raw materials that are not needed immediately, may delay purchases in raw materials that are needed for orders that can ship now.
- By motivating build to inventory rather than build to order. Putting product in inventory can improve profit *in the short run*, and it can also improve traditional metrics like utilization and efficiency. However, an order that can ship and be converting to cash may be waiting in queue behind product that is going to stock.
- By not applying a cost to the practice of dedicating resources in the form of machine time, materials, and labor to products that do not need to ship ahead of those that can ship immediately.
- By not valuing the cost of resources to make product that goes into inventory any different than those that go into product that can be converted to cash immediately.
- By using traditional product cost data to determine the cost–benefit of an investment, project, or customer. Projects that reduce lead time may be undervalued and therefore not authorized.

If your customers value lead time—and increasingly, time is becoming a factor in buying decisions, then you should consider how your product costing and metrics may be adding time to your entire process from order to cash.

Leading to the most important takeaway:

Customers do not like waiting

If you are using accounting practices or metrics that encourage long runs, overproduction, and building inventory—you are making your customers wait longer than necessary!

References

Balakrishnan, R., Labro, E., and Sivaramakrishnan, K. 2012a. Product costs as decision aids: An analysis of alternative approaches (Part 1). *Accounting Horizons* (March): 1–20.

Balakrishnan, R., Labro, E. and Sivaramakrishnan, K. 2012b. Product costs as decision aids: An analysis of alternative approaches (Part 2). *Accounting Horizons* (March): 21–41.

Bossidy, L. and Charan, R. 2002. *Execution—The Discipline of Getting Things Done.* New York: Crown Publishing.

Corbett, T. 1998. *Throughput Accounting.* Great Barrington, MA: The North River Press.

Goldratt, E.M. 1984. *The Goal.* Great Barrington, MA: The North River Press.

Horngren, C.T. 1977. *Cost Accounting—A Managerial Emphasis,* 4th edn. Englewood Cliffs, NJ: Prentice Hall.

Horngren, C.T. 2012. *Cost Accounting—A Managerial Emphasis,* 14th edn. Upper Saddle River, NJ: Prentice Hall.

Innes, J. and Mitchell, F. 1995. A survey of activity based-costing in the U.K.'s largest companies. *Management Accounting Research,* June 1995 issue: 137–153.

Innes, J., Mitchell, F. and Sinclair, D. 2000. Activity-based costing in the U.K.'s largest companies: A comparison of 1994 and 1999 survey results. *Management Accounting Research,* September 2000 issue: 349–362.

Johnson, H.T. 1992. It's time to stop overselling activity-based concepts. *Management Accounting* (September): 26–35.

Johnson, H.T. and Kaplan, R.S. 1987. *Relevance Lost—The Rise and Fall of Management Accounting.* Boston, MA: Harvard Business School Press.

Rother, M. and Shook, J. Foreword by Jim, W. and Dan, J. 2009. *Learning to See.* Cambridge, MA: Lean Enterprise Institute.

Rothschild, M. 2006. Shareholders pay for ROA—Then why are we still living in a margin-only world? *Strategic Finance,* November 2006 issue.

Stalk, G., Jr. and Hout, T.M. 1990. *Competing Against Time—How Time-Based Competition is Reshaping Global Markets.* New York: Free Press.

Suri, R. 1998. *Quick Response Manufacturing—A Companywide Approach to Reducing Lead Times.* New York: Productivity Press.

Suri, R. 2010. *It's About Time—The Competitive Advantage of Quick Response Manufacturing.* New York: CRC Press.

Suri, R. 2014. *MCT Quick Reference Guide.* Edgerton, WI: C&M Printing Inc.

Index